My Earliest Men

I was born on the 13th of April, 1928, at N
Grange, near Keith, on a croft of thirty
demobbed from the Black Watch in 1920. ㅠㄷ ㄸㄷㅖ ㅠㅇㅖㅖㅇㅁ ㅖㅇ ㅖ
miller with Syme Timber Merchants and Armstrong Timber Merchants
in Aberdeenshire, mostly in the Huntly area. He took over the lease
on the croft in 1927. My earliest memory is of my mother and father
going to Newmill, near Keith, where my father had a half-brother called
George Barclay. I was on a seat on the back of the bicycle when my
foot went into the wheel and was badly cut and bruised. They had to
cancel the trip and go back home and dress my wounds. The croft was
about two hundred yards off the main road and I used to go up there to
see all the children on their way home from school. After my accident I
had to crawl up the road to see them. I must have been just two or three
years old at the time. When I was about four, in the winter, I noticed
the school children all had sledges. I remember asking my father to
make one for me. I was too young to understand that he didn't have the
materials, far less the time, to do so. But I wasn't stuck. I found a bit
of old corrugated iron, about four feet by two feet, then a piece of rope
which I tied through holes in the iron. I was so proud of this sledge that
I took it up to the main road to show it to the school children. I can't
remember what they said but after I was a bit older, I realized they must
have had a good laugh at my efforts.

My brother David was born on the 4th of March, 1932. Someone came
to visit and asked me if I liked the new baby. I have no recollection of
what I said but apparently replied that he was no use to me until he
could crank the grindstone. I played with the grindstone quite a lot. It
measured about two foot six inches in diameter, set in a wooden frame
with a crank. I used to see how fast I could make it go. Thinking back
now, it was quite a dangerous ploy for a four year old boy.

Every Monday was the day the grocer's van came round. I always
got a cake of 'cow toffee', called that because there was a picture of a
cow on the wrapper. These were the only sweets we ever got because
my parents couldn't afford any more. Of course, I wished that every
day was a Monday. The baker's van came round on a Thursday and

sometimes I would get a fancy piece from it. My father kept quite a lot of hens and the eggs went to the grocer in part payment for the groceries. I didn't have many toys and any I did have would have been hand-me-downs. I did have a tricycle. I remember being over the moon when I got it. It came from my uncle George Barclay and had belonged to his children, all a good bit older than me. He was a guard on the railway and was a lot better off than my father with a weekly wage coming in. At Christmas a few parcels arrived containing presents from our relatives, usually sweets or a small toy. Then my father killed a few hens, the older ones I suspect. My mother plucked and cleaned then ready for the pot and that was what we gave to our relatives for their Christmas. A hen for Christmas dinner was a luxury then. Apart from that, Christmas Day and New Year's Day came and went just the same as any other day. I never heard of Santa Claus until I went to school. I wondered who they were speaking about.

As far as I can remember I was always happy with myself. We had about five cats, to keep down the vermin, and a black and white dog called Major I used to play with. He was supposed to be a collie but I don't think there was much of the collie breed in him. My father used to swear at him and said he was no use for anything. There was always a pig running about as well, a very friendly and petted beast. We had cattle too. I liked the calves which would suck my fingers when I held out my hand.

Another early memory I have is of a woman coming round the crofts with a creel on her back selling fish. I can just vaguely remember her but I heard my father speaking about her in later years. He said the creel was made from bamboo canes and built to fit comfortably on her back. She came from some of the fishing ports in the north east, possibly Buckie or Cullen. She would catch the coast train to Elgin, then the Aberdeen train and get off at Grange station. North Crannoch was about three miles from the station so that was quite a walk with a load of fish on her back. She sold the fish at houses as she went. I believe this was quite common all over the north east and, I suppose, other parts as well. I think that she must have been one of the last because I don't remember seeing them after I went to school. I also remember a tinker, Hugh Stewart by name. He came from Keith and used to travel round the farms every now and then with a sheltie and a cart. He would collect rags, rabbit skins, jars and brass and copper. My father always gave him a couple of sheaves of corn to feed his sheltie and mother would give him a cup of tea. Other tinkers came round but my father always kept everything for Hugh. I have vague memories of my father trying to break in a young horse. He jumped on it's back and it reared up and threw him off. I don't really know how badly hurt he was but his shoulder and arm were all tied up for some time. I don't think he would have gone to the doctor for treatment as doctors had to be paid then. On another occasion when my mother was coming down the road from one of the vans she lost half a crown, twelve and a half pence in today's money. There was snow on the ground and she spent what seemed to me to be a whole afternoon looking for it. I can't recall if she found it or not. She certainly could not afford to lose so much money. My father used to wear what we called 'tackety beets'. These were very heavy leather boots worn by all the country people. In fact when I left school and started work I also wore them. Father used to line the inside soles with straw which he changed frequently. This was common practice among farm servants. Nowadays we would just go to the nearest supermarket and buy new soles. I don't suppose it's possible to buy tackety beets now.

Some examples of the types of paraffin lamps we had

(above left) Eventually in the early 40s they managed to get a Tilly Lamp. That was a big improvement. (above right) This was the actual clock which sat on the mantlepiece as long as I can remember and when we got married, we didn't have a clock and this one had been replaced my father gave it to my wife with the words do not let him near it as he will just break it, him being me.

(above left) The kind of lamp my father used for the byre and stable.
(above right) Eventually he managed to upgrade to one called a Hurricane Lantern. I suppose it was called that because it could withstand the wind better.

(above left) This lamp would have been used mainly in the bedrooms.
(above right) and this one wold be mainly in the kitchen come sitting room.

My School Days at Crossroads School, Grange

I well remember my first day at school. My mother took me there, a distance of about a mile. When she went to leave I went berserk, shouting for her to come back. I was all right after a few days but from the first until the day I left I never liked school. I did have a lot of fun there though. The school teacher was called Miss Green. Back then the school books had to be paid for. Usually there were 'hand downs' which were cheaper. The desks were for two pupils with two separate lids under which we kept our sandwiches and spare pencils. On each side of the desk was an inkwell and pens and pencils. We had a slate for writing which slid into a slot in front of the desk with half of it left showing. There were about eighteen pupils in each class. Every room had radiators running off a big boiler fuelled by coke.

We had dry, outside toilets which didn't half stink. Mr. Leith, a local crofter, used to come periodically with his horse and cart and empty them. There were two playgrounds, one for girls and one for boys. If we were found in the wrong playground we got into trouble, usually the tag, which meant being struck on the hand with a leather strap. Across the road from the school was a shop, a general store, run by Mr. John Matheson. He had two daughters, Aileen, she looked after the shop, and Bella, who worked in an office in Keith. If any of the pupils had money they could buy sweets or whatever. Needless to say, I very seldom had any money. On the shop counter were always jars of sweets and sometimes, when Aileen had to go through the back, some of us would lift the jar lid and steal some sweets. Once when I was at this caper a girl called Myra Watt, an evacuee from Edinburgh, saw me through a small side window and blackmailed me so I had to hand over the sweets.

Sometimes my mother would give me a note to take some messages home from the shop and she would go down on Saturday and pay for them. I thought I would be fly and ask for a chocolate biscuit to be put on her account. She wasn't too happy but let me away with it until I got too greedy when she told the shopkeeper not to give me any more. I didn't understand how short of money my mother really was. I don't think she told my father about this or he would have strapped me with the leather belt he used for sharpening his cut throat razor. I can still feel that strap yet, but we were never punished unless we deserved it.

At the age of seven I was moved into the next classroom. Our teacher was a man called Harry Robertson. In this room was a big blackboard on two legs with four castors on the foot at the bottom of each leg. One day, two boys, John Pirie and Mackie Cowie and I were playing 'cars' pushing the big blackboard about when it tipped over and hit the piano, breaking a big chip off the wood at the top front left hand corner. When we tried to lift the blackboard back on it's feet it tipped the other way and landed on top of a desk, breaking the two slates in half. Well, we all got four of the tag for that and a letter to our parents asking for payment for the damage.

When my father saw that I got the belt from him as well, a bit more painful than the teachers tag. The next carry on happened when I was sitting at the back of the room. There was a glass fronted bookcase behind my desk. For some reason, I put my foot out behind my desk and my foot went through the glass and smashed it to smithereens. That got me another dose of the tag but it didn't have to be paid for and my parents never knew about it. Another time, when there was snow on the ground, I was playing in it with the small shovel used for sweeping the school floor when another boy did something to upset me. I swung the shovel at him, he dodged and the shovel went through a small window. Yes, I got the tag again. Some of us used to climb up on to the tower of the school building. A cast iron pipe ran from the ground up to a flat roof along the side and then up onto the tower. We were never caught doing this but someone could have easily been killed.

My brother was about six and I was about ten and we got up to a lot of pranks. We found a set of pram wheels and made a cart with them. There was a brae nearby, not very steep but enough for the cartie to run down. We took off down this hill, of course we had no means of stopping. We saw a car coming in the distance, I panicked and steered the cartie into the ditch. A bit of wire holding the cartie together was sticking up and caught David's arm. He got a very deep cut, about four inches long above his wrist and still has the mark to this day. I think he should have had it stitched but in those days you had to pay for treatment by a doctor so nothing was done. We also played with bikes which we made up from bits and pieces we found in dumps. I remember I had an old car steering wheel fixed on mine for handlebars and we went for a run one day. Someone had given us a penny each so we were off down to the shop. Coming from our croft to the crossroads shop was quite a steep brae and we didn't have much in the way of brakes. Half way down we came upon a herd of cattle. I managed to brake by putting my foot in between the tyre and the mudguard and was able to stop. David, who was out in front of me, couldn't stop and went flying down towards the cattle. I stood there absolutely terrified, sure he was going to be killed. I don't really believe in miracles but I saw one that day. A herd of fifteen or twenty cattle filled the road and somehow, they just opened up in front of him. He got right through without touching any of them. I can remember I sat down on the verge of the road, shaking with fear and shock. I don't recall if we managed to spend our pennies that day or not.

When I was about eleven years old, my father harnessed one of the horses for me to harrow between the turnip drills. I was getting on fine until I lost one of the reins. As a result the horse started to go around in a circle pulling all the turnips out. Eventually, I released my hold of the harrow, went to the horse's head and stopped it so I could get hold of the lost rein. Needless to say, my father wasn't too pleased and I never got the job again.

One of the highlights of the year was when the steam mill arrived to thrash the oats. Six or seven of our neighbours would come and lend a hand. Of course, my father went to help them when the mill went to thrash their crop. My mother always made a big pot of tattie soup which was the standard dinner for the steam mill day. I think the two men that worked the mill must have been pretty fed up eating tattie soup every day as they went round the farms in the district. They needed water for the steam engine so my father always opened up an old well and the water was carted to the engine in pails. I got that job at about the age of twelve although it usually took two of us to keep the engine supplied. After the mill left some of the chaff was used to stuff our mattresses. The filling was changed once a year. The chaff filled beds were so comfortable.

My first go at having my own business was making windmills. I used old syrup tins, cutting them into strips with my mother's scissors and twisting them. I then took some of my mother's kindlers, made a hole in the strips of tin and nailed them onto the kindlers. I sold the windmills to some of the other pupils, charging a half-penny each. Then some of the parents complained and I got a right telling off from the headmaster who told me to pay all the money back. The problem was I had spent it all, so my father had to stump up the money. I thought it was very unfair and still do.

The headmaster's name was George Fisher. 'Tag', should have been his middle name because most days it was, 'Baillie, come out here. Hold out your hand. No, not for a sweetie, the tag.' That reminds me about a singing teacher who came once a week to teach us to sing. Three of us refused to sing, Keith Runcie, John Pirie and I. We were mucking about when we should have been singing. She took us out to give us the strap. I was first in line. She gave me four smacks and asked if I'd had enough. 'No.' I said. I got another four smacks and she asked me again. Again, the answer was, 'No.' I got twenty two smacks in all. By that time the sweat was running off her forehead and the other two got off scot free. She had a wee car, an Austin, I think. The next week, at dinner time, we got our revenge. There was a field of turnips just across the road from the school. We pinched one and pushed chunks up the exhaust pipe. We kept pushing more and more up the pipe. As a result, the teacher had quite a problem trying to start her car. When it eventually fired, there was a big bang and all the bits of turnip shot out. There was no damage done. I don't think she would have known what was amiss.

A long time after, when I left the school, I would have loved to meet her again and say how sorry I was. Another time I remember when I had lifted my desk top and was having a bite of a sandwich when the desk top came down and banged me on the head. Fisher, the headmaster, had seen me and had thrown a book which hit the desk top and knocked it down on my head. What a fright I got. For a minute I wondered what had happened, then the shout came again, 'Baillie, come out here. Hold out your hand.'

Another highlight of the year was, of course, the school picnic. We were all bundled on to buses and transported off, usually to Cullen beach. We had games but what I remember most was the tea and sausage rolls and biscuits and the ice cream. It was a real treat because we would never see that at home. We had great fun running about the beach and paddling in the water. It would be another year before most of us would see the sea again.

I remember the first wireless we got. The Second World War had just started and my father wanted to keep up with its progress. We didn't have electricity, the wireless was powered with two batteries. One was a dry battery, about eight inches square and about three inches thick. When it went flat we had to fit a new one. We also used a small lead acid battery which had to be charged regularly. I remember the name of that wireless, it was called Blue Spot. I hadn't heard of that name before, nor since.

Back row from left to right, John Pirie, Lewis Rumbles, James Craib, Allan Stewart, Alex Shearer, Alex Stewart, John Cowie, Hugh Shearer. Middle row, Annie Paterson, Violet MacWilliam, Christina Davidson, Eva Irvin, Ella Duncan, Ina Duncan, Eleanor Dempster, Jess Shearer, Mary Milton. Front row, George Craib, myself, John Baillie, William Anderson.

In the summer holidays, when I was twelve years old, I got a job at a sawmill at Grange Station. The man in charge was, I think, Alex Lemon. My job was to stack the sawn timber. The mill belonged to Riddoch Timber Merchants, Tarryblake, Rothiemay. I was there for six weeks. I didn't want to go back to school as I now had my first wages but I had no choice. At tattie holiday time I got a job with Riddoch again. This time up on the Braco Hill, peeling felled trees. This could be dangerous, if you didn't watch as you turned the trees to peel the other side they would take off and slide

Crossroads School. The window I broke with the shovel was the bottom one. just to the right of the door. We climbed up the drainpipe on the corner of the tower to get to the top.

down the hill to the bottom. They reached such a speed that anyone in their path would have been killed. I took a few extra days off the school but nobody complained about that.

I also remember that all the school pupils went out and collected sphagnum moss. It was taken back to the school and two evenings a week we cleaned the moss and packed it into boxes to be sent off. The military used it to dress soldiers' wounds. I am not sure what it did but I think it had something to do with it being antiseptic.

I remember my father was going to Dufftown with a horse and cart to collect some furniture from my grandmother's house. She was moving in with Uncle George as she was too frail to live by herself any longer. I was on a bike going to the local shop for some messages for my mother, holding on to the cart, being pulled along when the front wheel of the bike went under the cart wheel and was completely wrecked. It was my mother's bike as well, so I didn't half get it from my father. What a temper he was in.

I used to go with my father to the moss to cut peats. As soon as we arrived among the heather the midges came out in their millions, queuing up to get a bite at us. I didn't like that one wee bit. The peat, when cut, was set out to dry and taken home later to be stacked up. Father had an old cart axle set in the ground with the wheel up. Some of the peat was set on this to dry. When the peat had all been burned in the fire, we had great fun using the wheel as a merry go round. We were easily amused in those days.

A salesman came to our house selling Jiffy Washing Machines and my father bought one. It was worked by hand. There was a paddle inside with slots through which the washing was placed. A shaft came up through the lid with a crank which you turned back and forth nearly a full circle. It was quite a hard job and didn't seem any easier than using the washing tub as before. It had a small wringer fitted on it which, I think, was the best bit. Mother used the machine all the time though.

There was a farm about a quarter of a mile from our croft, worked by Andrew Hay senior, Andrew Hay junior and Mrs Hay. They didn't keep a milk cow and father supplied them with milk. As it was on my way to school I used to deliver the milk in a small pail. I always got a biscuit, always the same kind, which they called a Fochie Biscuit. Long after, when I had left school, I realized why the biscuits got that name. There was a large bakery in Fochabers, called Murrays and it was one of their biscuits. They were a puff-pastry butter biscuit and I just loved them. You can buy similar biscuits today but none of them tastes as good as Murray's Fochie biscuits. Maybe over the years my taste has got a bit distorted.

The croft house where I was born and we were all brought up. The cart wheel bottom right is where the peats were stacked.

Part of the steading. The door you see was the barn where my father had a thresher driven by a paraffin engine. In the foreground is a binder which was used to cut the crops before the advent of the combine.

As you can see it was in a poor state of repair but the Fife estate would do few repairs to their dwellings. Downstairs was a kitchen come sitting room, a bedroom and a small room called the glory hole, just full of bits and pieces. A lean-to built on the back of the house was the milk house with one small window where the milk was kept as there were no fridges then. The floor of the kitchen come sitting room consisted of slate slabs laid on what would have been the original earthen floor. They were all shapes and sizes which didn't fit together very well and you could see the earth between them. We used to lift them and catch the earthworms underneath. A coal or peat fireplace was fitted with a swey, a piece of flat metal hinged vertically into the grate at one side with a horizontal piece welded on where pots and kettles could hang over the fire. The downstairs rooms were very damp, especially the bedroom, where the fire was only lit occasionally. Upstairs there were two bedrooms which were not damp as the whole upstairs was lined with tongue and grooved wood. This was actually the best part of the whole house. There was a porch built of corrugated iron. As you can see in the photograph, it was pretty rough. Just at the back of the door was the 'sink'. This was a barrel, cut in half. One half placed open end down on the ground and the other half on top, open end up. There was a hole cut in the bottom half and the bung in the top half was positioned to correspond with it.

The barrel sink

This is a swey with a cast iron frying pan and girdle

There was a cold water tap. On washing days, water had to be boiled on the kitchen fire. As for a toilet, well, there wasn't one. Not even a dry toilet outside as most folk in the country had. When you needed to go to the toilet it had to be the byre, or the nearest bushes. As bairns we never thought anything about it but now, I often wonder what our women relations did, and our many visitors.

I must have been about eleven when I went to see my first film. The film was Snow White and the Seven Dwarves. I was absolutely amazed. I had never seen anything like it. For a long time afterwards I thought there had been real people behind the screen. I don't know who paid for our trip to Keith but it was all organized by the school. I was so shy back then like most children brought up in the country. I think the reason was, when at home, we rarely had other children to play with. Children brought up in the town have friends most of the time and form groups or gangs. Although we had plenty of company at school it was more regimented. I wouldn't have changed it for a fortune.

There is something else I think I should mention and it's this. Although we had one of the best mothers we could ever wish for, I can never, ever remember her lifting her hand to punish any of us and only very occasionally did she raise her voice slightly to scold us. By the same token, I can never remember her giving me a hug or a kiss, although at the time I didn't think anything about that. She was very shy and she has passed that on to me. I think I know how she felt because to this day I feel uncomfortable about giving anyone a hug. It probably stemmed from her young days as she was brought up with a brother and sister, John and

Mother aged 12 in 1909

46 Years in One Job

Mr John Cruickshank, Home Farm of Lessendrum, Drumblade, who has been presented with the Highland and Agricultural Society's long service certificate and gold medal in respect of 46 years' continuous service with the Murray Bisset family.

Ann Cruickshank, at North Lodge, Lessendrum, Drumblade. She was born at Blackblair Farm, illegitimate daughter of Bella Alexander. Her grandmother, Isobel Mitchell, married John Cruickshank, John and Ann's uncle. Perhaps John and Ann, who were not really related to my mother, and never married themselves, didn't show her any affection. Nevertheless, she spoke very highly of them so I think they were very good to her in their own way. She had a quaint saying when things weren't going well, 'Dam' that weel a wite.' A very

Here she is aged 90 in 1987

John Cruickshank who brought up my mother. The photograph was taken when he was presented with a long service medal by the Bisset family of Lessendrum after being employed by them for forty-six years.

north east expression and as near to a swear word as possible without actually swearing.

My father used to tell us about when he and his brother, John, who worked at a distillery, used to run their motorbikes on whisky. Father didn't work at a distillery but got a supply from his brother, and probably some of the other distillery workers. They had what

Father in front of the porch with his collie, Flash.

they called a 'dog'. This was a length of copper pipe with an old penny, just over an inch across,

Photograph taken about 1908, of my grandparents' house, Easter Brawlands Croft, Kininvie, Dufftown. George & Ann Baillie, James Baillie and my father David Ballie. My grandfather, he died in 1920 aged eighty. My grandmother died in 1943 aged eighty-seven.

soldered to the bottom of the pipe, converting it into a container which was filled with whisky. A cork was then put into the top of the pipe with a length of string attached which then could be fixed to their braces and hung down inside the leg of their trousers. And that's how they managed to smuggle the whisky out of the distillery.

My father with his motorcycle.

I have mentioned a few times about my uncle George Barclay, my father's half brother. I didn't say that he was a survivor from the passenger ship Lusitania which was sunk by a German

My uncle, John Baillie.

torpedo in 1915 off the coast of Ireland. He had gone to Canada to make a better life for himself and managed to get work with a railway company. When he was settled with a job and had saved enough money he went back for his wife and that was when the boat was torpedoed. His home was in Newmill, Keith. In fact, he never went back to Canada. He got work with a railway company at Keith, was promoted as a Guard and was there until he retired.

Above me and my brother David. Note the suit which my mother made from an old overcoat and David's jersey, probably made with reclaimed wool. Left: My sister Agnes and my youngest brother, Gordon.

Sinking of the Lusitania. Keith Survivors Story

Keith survivors story. The steamer Lusitania torpedoed by a German submarine in May 1915 while sailing from New York to Liverpool. One of the survivor's was a George Barclay from Newmill, Keith, who had given up his railway job to seek his fortune in Canada. He was returning on the Lusitania to take his wife back with him to Canada. Below is a copy of his story to a local newspaper.

I do not want to go through the same experience again. I think I have been born under an unlucky star. Even in Canada I broke a leg. I was coming home to take out my wife if she will go but I won't go back until after the war. It was a very pleasant voyage, calm all the way. I never knew anything of the alleged warnings which I heard about when we landed in Queenstown. I got acquainted with one or two of the crew and joked about the boat being torpedoed but never thinking it would happen.

To tell the truth, I never thought the Germans would torpedo the boat. I put my watch to the ship's time, about 20 minutes to two o'clock and went up on deck. There, two of the boys were going down for a sleep and asked if I was going down. I said I would sit on deck and take my smoke. I was going to have a walk round the front part of the deck when she was struck by the first torpedo. I knew by the trembling of the ship that she was torpedoed. She listed and the crowd rushed the other way and carried me with them. Then the crowd went back and I went down for a lifebelt. A woman was there crying and I took off my lifebelt and strapped it on to her. I went into one of the boats but could not get it off and I got back on to the ship. The word got out that the ship was perfectly safe and not to lower any more boats. I was near the front part of the ship when there was another explosion. The ship had been struck by a second torpedo and splinters of wood etc. were flying in the air. I stood on the ship until she took the plunge and I sprang overboard. I was pulled down three times with the suction and the third time came up. I don't know whether it was wreckage but I could not get up and had to dive down again. And when I did get up I saw a black object in the water and started swimming for that which turned out to be a boat. I was very near there when a woman came floating past me crying for someone to save her, she could not swim. I got her on to the boat which was upside down, half scrambled on to it myself and we pulled thirty other men and women on to the boat.

One of the men had an arm off by the shoulder, crushed by two boats. Another man had three fingers torn off. We drifted about an hour and a half and every moment we thought the boat was going to be swamped. At length a cargo boat took us all on board. We arrived in Queenstown after dark. My watch was stopped at half past two, the time I ended up in the water. I do not for a moment think that the ship would have sunk if she had not got the second torpedo. We had to get clothes, we were told to go the drapery and get what we wanted. I did not want much, only a shirt, pants and a cap, but some were naked. I lost trunk, hand bag and everything. We stopped in Queenstown over Friday leaving at three o'clock, and I landed in Glasgow about nine o'clock on Sunday where I stayed until Monday morning. I saw one act of bravery by a woman. As far as I could see she swam back and forward and saved eight men and women. She looked to me to be one of the first or second class passengers. I don't know if she saved herself and I could not tell her face if I saw her again. It was pitiful to hear the cries of the women and children and if I had not been able to swim I don't suppose I would be here today.

My mother had started to serve her time with a dressmaker in Huntly after leaving school. Unfortunately, Ann Cruickshank, who had brought her up, died after a short illness and mother had to go home to look after John Cruickshank. Although she didn't qualify as a dressmaker she made good use of what she did learn. She used to go to any Bring and Buy sales, always looking for old overcoats and any woollen garments which she would unravel and wind into a ball to knit into clothes for us. It was no problem for her to make a suit from an old coat as there was ample material in an overcoat. As a result we were always smartly

(left) This picture of George Barclay was taken in Canada but as he lost all when the ship went down his photographs were lost along with all the rest of his belongings. His half brother, who had been in Canada since 1911 sent copies of any that he happened to have.

James Baillie, my father's twin brother sent George Barclay a copy of his photographs.

dressed. Any spare overcoats were used as extra blankets for our beds in the winter as she could not afford to buy blankets. Our diet consisted mostly of potatoes and milk, always in plentiful supply. We also enjoyed home made jam and cheese. Mother also baked scones, pancakes, oatcakes and sometimes fancy cakes such as rock cakes. The butcher's van came on a Saturday so Sunday was the only day we enjoyed beef for dinner. The stock from the cooked beef was used to make broth, usually enough for two or three days. At other times we would have stovies or 'chappit tatties', (mashed potatoes) with size (chives). From time to time we would get different kinds of home made soup using stock from a pheasant, shot by my father, or rabbits (always a plentiful supply). Sometimes there would be a hare, or perhaps a 'cushie doo' (wood pigeon). For our evening meal, supper as we called it, we mostly had birsled tatties (fried potatoes) with sausages or bacon and a bowl of milk. We never went to bed feeling hungry and that's the kind of food I still like to this day.

I remember my father's first tractor. He bought it from a chap by the name of Robbie Johnston. He had built it out of an old Ford 16 horse power car. It broke down in the middle of a field one day with some of the teeth stripped from the crown wheel on the back axle. Father managed to buy a replacement crown wheel and my brother David and I set out to change it. We got on well and had it changed in no time at all. When we started it up we discovered that we had three reverses and one forward gear. We had put the axle back on to the tractor upside down. We had no hope but to come home in reverse and then remove the axle and fit it the right way up. This machine was never much of a success and was eventually scrapped. I don't have a photograph of it but this is an artist's impression as I remember it.

Something else I remember. Apparently the Church of Scotland and the Free Church of Scotland in Grange were going to vote to be amalgamated. There was much disagreement between different families about whether this should or should not happen. The dispute became quite bitter. Families stopped speaking to one another, including my parents. Fights broke out at school among some of the older boys. It is something I could never understand. I have never believed in religion since and have got on pretty well without it.

North Crannoch Croft

Standen here far the barn eesed tae be
Far as a bairn I played and ran aboot wi' glee.
In the parks roon aboot wis stirkies and coos
An' fleein' aboot a puckle hungry doos.
Scratchin' aboot in the cornyard twa dizzen hens,
Faur they lay their eggs naebody kens.
Three or four cats roon aboot the rucks wis creepin'
For moosies and rats they were aye lookin'.
In the wee parkie, sooth o' the steadin'
Roads for the binder my feyther was redden.
Jist afore sax he wis oot o' his bed,
Twa coos tae milk and twa horses tae be fed.
And in the wee hoose far we a' eest tae bide,
A big open fire wi' a bink on ilkie side.
A cast iron kettle on a bink was sittin'
Hingin' fae the swey the hens pot was bilin'
At the table ma mither the tatties wis parin'
Wi' that bonnie floored overall she wis aye wearin'
The wa's o' the hoose a' mouldy wi' damp,
And on the dresser an auld paraffin lamp.
In ma mind's een I can see it a' yet,
And o' this a'm sure a'll ne'r forget.
Ower be the wee windae yonder
A pedal driven sewin' machine stood in the corner.
It wis gie well worn, it was used a lot.
Surprisin' fit she could mak oot o' an aul' overcoat.
A gie puckle years hiv noo geen past.
Aye, in them days the hooses were bigget tae last.
But noo, ower the grun the bulldozer has been,
A' that is left is just the wa's o' the hoose.
Naethin could bide there, nae even a moose.
That wis the craft far we wis a' reared.
Bit noo the hale lot his a' disappeared.

Jock Baillie

1941 I Started Work

At the end of June, 1941, when the school holidays started, I got a job with James Clarke, of Fortrie, Grange. I was thirteen years and two months old. I applied for and got an exemption, which was available when we were thirteen and six months old, if we went to work on a farm. I should have gone back to school after the holidays until September 13th. In fact I never did go back to school and nobody ever asked why. My wage was thirty-six pounds for the half-year. Every week we got what we called a 'sub' of ten shillings and the remainder at the end of the six months. At the farm I lived in a room called 'the chaumer', in Banffshire, and in Morayshire called 'the bothy'. This was a small room built into the steading as accommodation for the hired hands. The foreman, Jock Leslie, and a bloke by the name of Shearer also stayed in the chaumer. The men got their meals in the farmhouse kitchen. For breakfast there was a big bowl of oatmeal on the table, salt and spice, a kettle of newly boiled water, a jug of cream and a small bowl for each of us to make brose. We put a handful of oatmeal into our bowls with some salt and spice to taste, added boiling water and mixed it to a thick paste. Also on the table was a pot of tea, a slice of bread for each of us and butter and jam, which was just as well as I did not like the brose very much. I always took some so as not to be the odd one out. Since I left that farm I have never, ever, eaten brose again. We always got a good dinner at mid-day, this was usually fine, thick farmhouse soup, and for supper, a fry up.

The farm was owned by the Clarke family. James Clarke was semi-retired, most of the work done by his son, also James. His other son, Sandy had been kicked on the head by a horse when he was a toddler leaving him severely brain-damaged. I don't know where he slept but he had to take his meals with us in the kitchen. He was prone to wandering away from home and would go round the neighbouring crofts where he would ask, 'gie us a piece, ye bugger,' (give me a piece of bread). His pockets were always bulging with slices of loaf and biscuits although he got plenty to eat at home. His next request would be, 'gie us a penny, ye bugger, nae a white penny, a broon penny.' There were two more Clarke brothers, Dod, (George) and Beel (William). The brothers were all over six feet tall, very well built and had all been in the police at one time. George was a professional wrestler but was always billed as coming from Dundee. Sandy was a crack hand at mocking people and brilliant at imitating auctioneers. I was not long there when I was sent round the edge of a field and told to cut the thistles. Much later on when the crops were ready to be harvested they had to cut a road round the edge of the field with a scythe for the binder. Someone then had to lift the stalks of corn and bind them into sheaves. I was sent to do that because the farmer said I had not made a good job of cutting the thistles. By the end of the day my hands were full of stabs and very sore. I decided that this job was not for me and told the farmer I was leaving. He flew into a rage and chased me round the close with a binder canvas he was repairing. I really thought he was going to kill me. Once he went back into the house I grabbed my belongings from the chaumer and went home. He still owed me twelve pounds which I never got, or at least he didn't realize I got it years later. This happened in 1961 when I was running my own business. He came to see me and ordered 150 tons of gravel. As I made out his account, I made sure I got my twelve pounds, plus interest.

My next job was for six weeks, the duration of the harvest. The farm, near Fordyce, was called Drakemyres and owned by Mr. Cowie. I was living in the chaumer and my only complaint was the place was alive with rats. Through the night I could feel them running across the foot of my bed. There wasn't a light that I could switch on so I just tucked my head under the blankets and stayed there until morning. I managed to stick it out for the six weeks. After that Mr. Cowie sent me to see Mr. William Rust at Bogmuchals. He had horses hired to the forestry and I got a job with a horse dragging trees. It was a big Clydesdale with a white face shaped like a star, hence his name, Starry. He wasn't a very good horse because whenever he got the chance he would run off back down to his stable. I tried leaving the reins trailing so that he would stand on them but he soon got wise to that and would hold his head to one side. One day he made to take off, I managed to catch the reins and gave them a bad tempered tug. Up he reared and came down on top of me, hitting me on the chin with a front hoof. I was knocked flying. The horse took off home while I was lying dazed, blood dripping from the wound on my jaw. I didn't even have a hankie so I picked a docken leaf and held it to my jaw until it stopped bleeding. I still have the mark to this day. I really should have had a couple of stitches in it. Mr. Rust said, 'I don't think you are able for that horse.' I agreed. He tried Starry with an older man, Mr Aitken, but he had the same problem with the horse running home. It was only three weeks until Starry reared again and came down on Mr. Aitken's head, fracturing his skull. Mr. Rust's son, William, then took charge of Starry. He was a big, well built chap and probably more able to master the horse.

At that time I travelled to work from Grange. Our neighbours next door, David and Joe Robb, were brothers who also worked at Greenhill. Joe and I bought a motor bike between us, a 350 Ariel. As we couldn't buy petrol because it was rationed, we filled the carburettor with lighter fuel to get it started. The tank was filled with tractor paraffin and we managed to run it with that. We didn't have road tax or insurance. The rod for working the back brake was missing but we managed to get over that by attaching a rope to the lever on the back wheel and tied it to a tank bracket at the front. When we wanted to brake we just put a hand down and pulled the rope. That worked pretty well until one day a deer ran on to the road in front of us. In a panic, Joe grabbed what he thought was the rope but caught the plug lead instead and pulled it out of the magneto. The bakelite part on the magneto broke and we landed in the ditch. Neither of us was hurt but my two thermos flasks in my piece bag were broken and that was the end of the motorbike.

After that I went into the camp of The Home Grown Timber Production Department. They were harvesting the trees at Greenhill and I got a job there. About eighty per cent of the workforce were women. About fifteen of the men who stayed there had originally worked in the forest of Langanburn. I believe that was a horrendous place to work, very wet and mossy. Although I never worked there I heard plenty of stories about horses sinking up to their bellies in the wet ground and of men getting stuck in the moss. One story was told of a tractor disappearing into the moss never to be seen again. Whether that was true or not I can't tell but by all accounts it was a difficult place to work and, I believe, eventually parts of it were abandoned.

We were transported by lorry from the lodge to Green Hill. The lorry driver came from Dundee and his truck was a Ford Thames V8 petrol engine. I think the battery must have been faulty. He always had to crank it to get it started in the morning, to my great amusement. He would go and blow into the petrol tank, then run round and crank the handle. He had to go through this procedure two or three times before the engine would start. I had been there about six weeks when we were moved to a camp at Oathillock. This was a wooden hut with a cook house near by where we got our meals. We were really well fed and I had no complaints. For breakfast we had porridge, bacon and egg and if that was not enough there was always bread, jam and tea. For dinner at midday we had sandwiches which the cook made to take with us. At supper there would be mince and potatoes, stovies or mashed potato with chives, or maybe potato soup. Sometimes we had stew with potatoes and vegetables and we always got pudding as well. I always remember a funny incident that happened one supper time. In the camp was a man called Frank Adams, a lorry driver from Forgue. The pudding this particular night was rice pudding and he found a small piece of wire in his. He told the cook, 'I don't mind eating concrete, but to hell with it when it's reinforced.' At the time I thought it was very funny.

I was given the job as a loader, along with some of the girls loading pole bogies and slipes (sledges) for the tractors to pick up and deliver to the sawmills. Eventually I was given the job as second man to a George Grant, from Cornhill. He drove a Fordson petrol tractor. I really enjoyed that job as he was a very nice man to work with. He had one amusing peculiarity and I couldn't help watching him, when he was smoking a cigarette he continually rolled it with his tongue from one side of his mouth to the other. I eventually got a tractor to drive myself, an International TD6 Crawler. Because it was a crawler I was sent to any of the wet parts of the forest where there were big spruce trees. They thrived better in wet ground. I had two Timber Jills with me as loaders. Betty Wilson, from Lincoln and Sheila Dewar, from the Edinburgh area.

As I was only fifteen years old the gaffer, Jimmy Stewart, told me that if anyone asked what my age was I should say I was seventeen. In fact nobody ever asked me how old I was. There were three sawmills, one at Airdiecow on the north side, one on the east side at Heathcote and one on the south side at Newbiggins. I hauled timber to any of the three mills. The smaller timber, suitable for pit props, we delivered to the road side to be loaded on to lorries and driven to the nearest railway station. There they would be loaded on to railway wagons and delivered to the coal mines as pit props. Betty Wilson nicknamed me Sunshine because

This is a caterpillar D4 which I drove for a short time. Betty Wilson and Sheila Dewar are on the tractor.

Some more timber workers I worked with at Loch Loy.

she said I was always smiling and that name stuck with me for the rest of my time in the timber trade. There was also a light railway supplying the Airdiecow sawmill. The engine was a three cylinder Ruston. The railway track was on a steep slope as it approached the sawmill and the slightest drop of rain would cause the engine to slip on the rails, gathering speed all the time. The driver would usually jump off and let her go. This happened once with four or five Timber Jills hitching a ride. When the engine took off they all jumped except one, Madge Hastings. She had frozen, quite terrified. The driver stayed with her, trying to get her to jump but by this time the engine was going too fast. It smashed into the buffers at the bottom where it overturned, trapping Madge underneath. They eventually got her out and except for a few bruises, she was none the worse. These engines were fitted with boxes filled with sand with pipes emptying about an inch from the rails. If you worked a lever, sand would trickle onto the rail and give the wheels a grip. It didn't always work, a common cause being the sand was damp. After that accident the railway was never used again.

I remember there was a marquee dance in a field near Bogmuchals and as I'd gone home to Grange for the weekend I decided to cycle down. I was so shy then it was unbelievable. They quite often held dances in the Grange Memorial Hall and more than once I had cycled there fully intending to go in but every time I got there I just could not face going in. After once or twice of this carry on I just stopped going. This seemed to be a problem with anybody brought up in the country although I was exceptionally so. This time, however, I met up with a girl I knew because she was a maid at Fordyce Lodge where the timber department had its office. Other people lived in other parts of the lodge and she worked for them. I thought I would ask to walk her home but there was another bloke keen on her as well, Sam Davidson, by name. Nevertheless, she went with me and when we got to the lodge she said, 'I'll go inside.' She pointed to a window and said, 'That's my room. I'll go in and open the window and you can jump in.' So off she went. I was thinking this is a bit dangerous, so I took off and went back to the marquee to get my bicycle. Ah, but when I got there both my tyres were flat. Sam Davidson had taken out both the valves and thrown them away. There was nothing for it but to walk home, a distance of seven miles.

There was a fancy dress dance billed for the hall at the village of Berryhillock and some of the Timber Jills wanted to dress me up for this. Being shy I wasn't keen and didn't want to go to the dance. Eventually they persuaded me to go. They dressed me up as a Chinese man complete with a long pigtail down my back. I don't know where they got the pigtail, maybe they cut it off a horse. Anyway I fair enjoyed myself that night, and I won a prize.

At the camp at Bogmuchals there was a hut for trainee Timber Jills. Here they were given practical training before being posted to different localities. On one occasion, when they were out learning how to fell trees the supervisor had to leave them to go down to the office. When she came back there was no sign of the trainees. She eventually found them some distance away in the forest where they had started felling trees. The trees they felled were all hung up on the standing trees and they were in a right mess. They got a proper telling off for that and a day's pay stopped. Among the trainees were two sisters from Glasgow, Isa and Sadie McMullan. It's not unusual to hear women swearing nowadays but not back then, not in public anyway. Those two sisters just let rip. I've not heard women swearing so much as those sisters. They were so annoyed at losing a day's pay.

Isobel Thain was the camp cook and orderly and I rather admired her. I really wanted to ask her out but I was far too shy and nothing would have allowed me to ask her for a date. Unknown to me, however, she also fancied me. One evening I was late in for my supper and when I had finished I went to go back to the hut. Isobel came to the door with me and started making conversation. She said there was a concert down at Berryhillock Hall and she had nobody to go with, would I accompany her. In fact we never did go to that concert but we did go out nearly every night after that. I was sixteen and she was eighteen. She was my first girlfriend and I was her first boyfriend. We went out together for about a year and then got engaged. One day we took the train from Keith to Aberdeen, the fare cost about four shillings return each, and I bought her a ring. She also bought a ring for me, silver with a heart and our initials entwined. I can't recall what her ring looked like. We went out together for about another year and then we fell out. I know now that it was just as well that we split up because I was far too young and immature. I don't think our relationship would have lasted, but we did have a lot of good times and I wouldn't have liked to miss it. I knew it was final when she sent the ring back and from that day on I never saw or heard about her. When I was stationed in Germany with the army I exchanged her ring for a camera.

Early in 1944 Greenhill was all finished and we were moved to Lochloy near Nairn. We stayed in a camp at Dallas called Edinvale. There was a hut for the men and across the road one for the women. We travelled to Lochloy in a lorry driven by Robert Reid. Isobel Thain was cook and camp orderly and had an assistant, Mrs McHard, to help look after both camps. I got the job driving the light railway engine, the 'puggie', on a line about three miles long. The engine I was driving was a Ruston Diesel and the other was a Simplex Petrol, pulling four bogies each. At the end of the railway loaders would put the logs on to the bogies and we would collect them and leave other bogies for them to load. When we reached the main road we left the full bogies for the workers to unload and we took the empty ones away. The logs were then loaded on to lorries and taken to the sawmill at Darnaway. The logs to be used as pit props were taken to Brodie or Forres Station to be loaded on to railway wagons heading for the coal mines. One time I was coming up with a load and the other puggie was coming down pushing the empty bogies. The driver was supposed to go into one of the sidings with the empty wagons to let the loaded one pass. I stopped but he kept on coming. Too late, he saw me and tried to stop but couldn't. The empty bogies crashed into my engine and went flying all over the place. It turned out that he'd been on the booze the night before and had fallen asleep. If he hadn't seen me at the last moment it would have been a lot worse, but nothing was broken. The empty bogies were all off the rails, it took us about an hour to get them back on again.

We always worked for half the day on a Saturday and my girlfriend, Isobel Thain got every second weekend off. She used to come with me on the puggie, just for the run. On Saturday afternoon we all piled on the lorry which took us all home like a bus service. Some workers were dropped off in Elgin then on to Buckie, round the coast to Cullen then up to Keith, dropping me off at Grange before going on to Huntly. Quite a few of the men stayed there. At times I came off the lorry at Buckie and spent the weekend with Isobel's family. Sometimes she would come to Grange and stay at my home. Early in 1946 the girls began to get demobbed so Isobel left and got a job as a clippie on the buses. She didn't like it very much and it was shortly after that we fell out. We were walking up to her house at Hill of Maud when we had a serious quarrel. I turned and went back to Buckie, she carried on to her home and I never saw her again. Shortly afterwards I heard that she had left the buses and got a job as a domestic servant at Broomhill Farm, Fordyce.

The gaffer at Lochloy was James MacDonald who lived in a house at Brodie, just across from the railway station. Everybody knew him as Tackets, and he was well liked by all the workers. Some time before we were moved there a squad of forestry workers from Newfoundland had been harvesting the trees. Their accommodation huts were about half a mile into the forest. It was pretty basic, all built with slabs from the sawmill. I could never understand why it was so far from the main road. Down near the beach were sand dunes, actually part of Culben Sands. The sand was continually moving with the wind. A sapling would be there one day and gone the next but another one would have appeared somewhere else. Since then I think some kind of grass has been planted to help stop the sand from blowing. Once a week the truck was laid on to take us down to Forres where we could go to the pictures or play billiards. There was a pub where we went to play darts. I was in the darts team and we played against the other teams from Forres and the area around the town.

My Army Days

I got my calling up papers about the 20th of April, 1946, and was told to report to Retford Barracks, Worksop, Nottinghamshire and be there by the 2nd of May. My address at that time was Edinvale Forestry Camp, Dallas so my train pass was from Forres Station. On reaching Worksop Station I found another twenty-five or thirty men waiting for transport to Retford Barracks. Soon a truck appeared to take us to the

Isobel Thain

Even more
Timber Jills.

camp. On arriving we were given empty palliasses which we had to fill with with straw from a nearby hut. On we went to another hut where we were given two blankets each and that was our beds catered for. Next we had to go to the Quartermaster's store to collect our uniforms. Here we walked in a line along beside a counter with soldiers behind it. They literally threw the clothes at us, trousers first, then jackets and shirts. They asked my neck size, well, I didn't have a clue about that so they threw across the first shirt they laid their hands on. Then they asked my hat size, again I didn't know so, once again, the first one that came to hand was tossed over to me. Then socks and lastly boots. At least I knew the size of my feet. After that we went back to our Nissen hut to make up our beds. All the beds had pillows on them but for some reason there was no pillow on mine. I nipped in to the hut next door which was empty and took a pillow off a bed. Ah, but someone saw me and I got one hell of a row from the Sergeant. He said that I might have been a thief in civilian life but they would not tolerate thieves in H.M. Forces. I had to put the pillow back and go to the Quartermaster's store for another one. I was interrogated by a Sergeant there as well about what happened to the pillow in question. 'What the hell have I landed in here?' I wondered. There was a tailor in the camp and we were sent to him to get our clothes altered to fit. We had to visit the barber next to have our hair cut and he didn't leave us with very much. Next day we had to go and get all our webbing equipment, no problem there. Then to the armoury to be issued with rifles.

The day after that all hell broke loose. We were divided into different companies and set to marching up and down, back and forth and round about. The real shambles came when given the order, 'Right turn.' Some went right but others turned left, some even turned right round. One man had a peculiar way of marching where instead of his arm going back when his leg went forward it always went the same way as his leg. They had some job getting him to march properly. I was always of the opinion that he was trying to work his ticket, but I don't know if that really was his game. As time wore on our marching improved although it didn't stop the Sergeant from shouting and bawling at us. There was one episode I remember very well, a man from Paisley and I were mucking about and he banged into me. My rifle landed on the ground and you would have thought we had committed murder, the way the Sergeant reacted, ranting and raving. He made us go and get a fire pail each, fill the pail with stones and go right round the yard at the double carrying these pails of stones. It was a fair distance to go and before I got round I was just about beat. 'I'm just about there.' I thought, and then the bastard said, 'Go round again.' The second time I just walked round, I just couldn't do it at the double. Nor could my mate from Paisley. In the evening we had to paint all the webbing with Blanco and polish our boots until we could see our faces in them. We used the handle of a toothbrush to burnish them. Every morning we had to fold our blankets and lay them on our beds. Our webbing equipment had to be laid out to be inspected by a sergeant who never failed to find something wrong. After lights were out at 10 o' clock we were not supposed to speak but another soldier and I were whispering and the sergeant heard us. He took us out to the middle of the floor and told us to hold our rifles above our heads with both hands and mark time until he told us to stop. I don't know how long it was but I was forced to stop. I just could not go on any longer. He sent us back to our beds and said he didn't want to hear one word out of us for a week.

We also had to be seen by the dentist and my teeth were in a pretty bad state. When I was at school nobody told us to clean our teeth and I can't remember ever seeing a toothbrush in our house. The result was that most of my teeth were rotten by the time I was seventeen. The dentist was horrified but said he would try to save them. He filled most of them but had to remove some. Next day I had a desperately sore face, my jaw had become infected. I should have reported sick but didn't. My jaw got worse and apparently, in the middle of the night, I was raving with a very high temperature. Some of my mates roused a corporal who stayed in one of the small rooms in the hut used by the NCOs. He fetched a doctor who then called an ambulance which took me to the Victoria Hospital Military Ward in Worksop. A surgeon operated on my neck to drain all the poison off and I was given penicillin injections. When I was released after twelve days the doctor told me the operation was nearly too late. Another hour and the poison would have gone all through my body.

Once I was back in training again we were taken to the shooting range. I had a problem with that too. My right eye is weak and always has been. At home when I used to go shooting rabbits with my father's shotgun I always fired from my left shoulder. I explained this to the Sergeant and asked if I could fire from my left shoulder. 'No way.' he said. As ordered, I fired from my right shoulder and needless to say, I missed the target altogether. I was sent for a medical, my eyes were tested and they found I had a scar on my right eyeball. This meant I was downgraded from A1 to A3, but by this time my posting came through for the Oxford and Bucks Regiment as a rifleman. I was not very pleased about being posted to an English regiment. Anyway, that was cancelled of course because of my eyesight and I got a new posting, this time to Cirencester in Gloucestershire to start training with the Royal Army Service Corps. That was very different from Retford where we mostly did square-bashing. I was very glad to get away from that place but I suppose they had to install some discipline into us. In Cirencester we were in a classroom most of the time. Some of the things we learned were how to read a micrometer, how to magnetize a magnet and map reading, things like that. We still had to go on parade and keep all our equipment up to standard. There would be an inspection parade periodically and many of us were caught out not keeping our rifles clean. The Sergeant would look down the barrel and sure enough he would find the tiniest speck of dust. The Nissen huts that were our billets had a long passage leading to the room where we all slept. Off the passage were small rooms, two for NCOs and one for equipment. One night when I was sound asleep some of my mates lifted me and my bed out into the passage. I hadn't felt them doing this but in the morning I was half awake when I saw this figure coming towards the bottom of the bed. I couldn't understand why he kept on coming up to my bed and didn't stop. He came clattering on top of me. I wondered what had happened. It wasn't long before I found out it was the Duty Sergeant coming to waken us. As he had come in from the half-light he couldn't see the bed. He hurt one of his legs and, oh what a rage he was in. He was just dancing with rage. He bawled out, 'What the bloody hell do you think you are doing sleeping in the passage?' The whole lot of us were confined to barracks and told we would be there until the culprits confessed. I don't think he made it official because it was all forgotten about in a few days.

After that I was posted to Salisbury for fourteen days to train as a TMT storeman (Tradesman Motor Transport). Then back to Cirencester and shortly afterwards I was posted to Germany. We sailed from Harwich to the Hook of Holland. While we were waiting for the order to board the ship we were all assembled and a Staff Sergeant called for all soldiers with surnames starting with the letter A and B to step forward. We were assigned to guard duty because down in some of the holds were German prisoners being repatriated. Many of them didn't want to go home. One of them said to me he had nothing to go home to, all his family had been killed and there was no house left. Many of their homes were in the Russian zone and there was no way that they would want to go there. We had to stand guard at the top of the hatches to stop them jumping ship. I can certainly say that was the worst journey I have ever had in my life. We were little more than a mile out to sea when I was violently sea sick. I vomited all down the barrel of my rifle and ended up with a German prisoner holding my rifle while I was at the side spewing into the sea. I was so sick that I couldn't have cared less if I had fallen overboard into the sea. The duty period was one hour on two hours off and I didn't have to go on duty again. I expected to get into trouble for giving the German my rifle but I didn't. Either the guard commander didn't see it happening or he didn't bother challenging me. I was not the only soldier by any means to be sea sick but I think I was the worst affected. I made up my mind then that if anyone ever asked my surname again I would say 'Wilson'. We eventually landed at Hook of Holland where we boarded a train bound for a transit camp at Hannover. We stayed there until our posting came through for whatever unit we would be assigned to. In the meantime I got talking to a German lassie working in the cookhouse and we went out together for the four weeks I spent there. A very nice girl, her name was Yutta Von Heitage.

Yutta Von Heitage

Autobahn taken from the back of a truck.

About the second day I was there I went for a walk with two other soldiers into the town. There wasn't very much to see as it had been badly bombed. We came across a cafe kind of place, I'm still not sure what it was. A notice outside read, 'Out of Bounds to all UK Military Personnel.' Still, we went in and were sitting at a table drinking what was supposed to be Kartoffel Schnapps, which is alcohol distilled from potatoes. I didn't like it very much and had only taken a couple of mouthfulls when I went to the WC. As I was coming back out I saw two Military Policemen coming in through the cafe door. I shot back into the WC. There was another soldier there, I didn't know him but as soon as he spoke I knew he was Welsh and his shoulder flash said Hussars. I said, 'M.P.s just coming in the door of the cafe.' 'I can't afford to be caught.' he said. 'I've already been caught a short time ago.' He tried to open the window but had no joy there. He lifted his foot to knock out the bottom pane of glass but the whole frame, glass and all, fell out. It must have been rotten. He jumped out and when he landed I did hear a bit of a grunt. I waited a second or two to give him time to get out of my way and then I jumped as well. Because it was dark we didn't know there was an eight foot drop below the window. He was still trying to get up when I landed on top of him. Then we couldn't find a way out, it was someone's back garden and there was a dog that kept barking and barking. Eventually we did get out and got to an area that was lit. We could see his hands were all covered in blood, cut with the broken glass. I was lucky because I had landed on top of him and not the window I only had one small cut to my hand. The other two lads that were with me both got ten days CB (confined to barracks). This meant they couldn't go out as they had to report to the guardroom every hour. When my next posting came through it was for No. 10 Independent Station Maintenance Section at Brunswick. I was really lucky to get that posting because it was so laid back with no guard duties or anything like that. The officer in charge was a Captain. As for the rest of us, there was a Staff Sergeant, a Sergeant, a Corporal and eight Privates. There were two auto electricians, one office worker, a cook, three motor mechanics and I was the storeman. We looked after about thirty German workers as well. They were still in the German Army, known as the Disarmed German Army.

Although we were in barracks with a workshop, our unit was actually a mobile workshop and we did periodically go out on exercises, always with other units. We did all the maintenance and repairs for other units such as the Royal Medical Corps, the Royal Army Ordnance Corps and quite a few motor cycles for despatch riders, to name but a few. I also got in tow with a girl, Gerda Bertram and we went out together for the three months or so we were there. Not long after I started dating her she asked me home to meet her parents and her brother. That was the first and last visit to that family. Her father and brother were proper Nazis, real Gestapo material I'd say. Gerda was like a lot more German girls, just out for what they could get like cigarettes and chocolate. In a way you couldn't blame them as they couldn't buy these things. One cigarette on the black market cost seven marks.

The winter of 1946/47 was very severe with terrible frosts. We woke up one morning and the floor down the centre of the barrack was covered with a sheet of ice. A pipe had burst through the night, something to do with the central heating, which had been turned off. It was like being inside a fridge and by evening the heating had not been restored. One of the auto electricians, Jonny Hudson, took in a motor battery and a twelve volt bulb. He put the bulb inside one of his socks and put it in his bed. Ten minutes later smoke started coming from underneath the blankets. He pulled the blankets down to find his sock was burned to a cinder and the blankets all scorched. We all had a good laugh at his expense but I don't recall Jonny laughing very much. Sometimes we went on an exercise, usually about three weeks duration. We always went with other units and we had to cater for all the breakdowns. I was one of the squad on the breakdown truck on one exercise and we ended up towing twenty one broken-down vehicles and that was a real headache. With so many vehicles being towed at once turning a sharp corner meant the ones in the middle tended to cut the corner and land in a field.

(far left) I'm at Gutersloh Aerodrome, Germany, 1948. Photograph of us out on an exercise and, no, we didn't have hot water for washing. This is us doing our ablutions first thing in the morning. Note the water bowser in the background for water supplies. That's me on the right. For cooking we had to dig a shallow trench about eight feet long, place a flat sheet of metal on top of the trench and use a massive great kerosene blow lamp at one end with the flame going through the trench. This heated the metal sheet and the cooking pots were placed on top. (left) Myself at Gutersloh Areodrome, Germany 1948. (center) Jonny Hudson who set fire to his bed. He was from Leeds. (right) The Sergeant who issued me with my driving license is in the middle. I'm on the left. (far right) Gerda Bertram from Brunswick.

We were all taken to see Belsen Concentration Camp. I think most of the soldiers had to go and see one of the camps. There wasn't much to see, it had all been landscaped with signs where the huts and gas chambers had been.

To get home for leave we were transported to a transit camp at Bellfield. We stayed there overnight then got a train to Hook of Holland and boarded a troop ship to Harwich. A train took us from there to Liverpool Street Station then tube to King's Cross and the train to Aberdeen. That was really a desperate journey, the whole corridor was full of soldiers sitting on their kit bags or lying on the floor. At York Station a lot of passengers got off so I was lucky and found a seat. After we reached Glasgow there was plenty room. We got into Aberdeen about 10pm but there was no connection to Keith until morning. In every major railway station in the UK the Railway Transport Office was manned day and night by military personnel so I went to enquire about a train for Keith in the morning. I spoke to a Corporal, he told me the time of the train but also said that the post office trucks were loading mail from the train I had just got off and that I might get a lift to Keith on the truck heading north. The driver said it would be no problem, he did this quite often. We got to Keith about 4am and I then had to walk to Grange, about eight miles, carrying my kitbag. By the time I got home I was really in need of my bed. The Railway Transport Officer (RTO) was very helpful. One time when coming home from Bellfield again I didn't read the notice board, I didn't think there was any need, but if I had I would have learned that the time for the train departure had been changed to one hour earlier resulting in my missing the train. I found out from a Non Commissioned Officer (NCO) that I was not alone. He told me to go to the RTO at Harwich railway station and they would stamp my pass with the date I arrived there, hence I could take a day longer at home and not lose any of my leave.

My next move was to a small town called Wolfenbuttel. The camp was occupied by the Hussars, a tank regiment. Our base was a workshop within the premises. We now had a different CO, Captain Ganner, a really nice chap. We could have run about half naked and he would not have bothered about it. After breakfast we had to parade, nothing regimental, more or less to see that everyone was there. More than once I went on parade still eating my breakfast. I still didn't have a driving licence then but while talking to a Sergeant one day the conversation got around to driving. I mentioned I didn't have a driving licence. 'Can you drive?' he asked. 'I think so.' I replied. 'Jump into that truck, (a QL Bedford truck) and we'll go down the town and have a cup of tea at the Church of Scotland canteen.' Well, that cost me the price of a cup of tea and three doughnuts and that was the only driving test I've ever had.

Shortly after that I went on a course to learn to be a mechanic. I passed that then became a driver mechanic. We usually only did running repairs, not major jobs such as complete engine overhauls or gearbox repairs. Big jobs like those were all sent to the Royal Electrical Mechanical Engineers. They had a big depot at Celle and that was where our MT stores got spares to keep up their stock along with oxygen and acetylene bottles used for welding.

Mobile workshop trucks Machinery wagon equipped with a lathe, vertical drill, welder and valve grinder. Cooking facilities, tents etc. Stores carrying a selection of truck spares Scammel recovery truck, also a water bowser.

I wasn't long in Wolfenbuttel when I became friendly with a lady called Margaret Brands, a really very nice girl. I kept company with her all the rest of my time in Germany. She was actually married but her husband was a prisoner of war in Russia and had written telling her that he was going to stay in Russia. Long afterwards I read that German prisoners in Russia were forced to write to their families saying they didn't want to come home. In fact they were used as slave labour. Over the years I have often wondered if he ever did come back to Germany. She often spoke about her father who was a soldier as well. It was thought he had managed to escape from Berlin as the Russians overran the city. Someone had seen him hanging

Margaret Brands, my girlfriend from Wolfenbuttel, Germant.

on to the door of a tramcar full of people trying to flee from the Russian advance but he was never seen or heard from again. He had been a farmer before he was called up. One of thousands of similar stories. Wolfenbuttel was a smashing town to be stationed in. It hadn't been bombed because there were no factories. The camp was just great. The Hussars manned the guardroom and we didn't have to report when going out or coming in, they just waved us past. We were supposed to go into our office and sign in and out but nobody bothered. There was a cinema in the town it was run by ENSA (Entertainment National Services Association) and a Church of Scotland Canteen which was really first class. A lot of the cookies were home baked and their home made soup was really good. I spent the bulk of my pay there. There was also a NAFFI van which came round to our workshop in the morning and then again in the afternoon with tea and cakes, My favourite being doughnuts, piping hot, just out of the pot. I can taste them yet.

We did a lot of repairs to motor cycles and managed to salvage enough parts to build a motorcycle to go scrambling with. We got a lot of fun out of that and were in the process of collecting enough parts for another one when our unit was disbanded and we were all posted to different companies. I was posted to 54 Co. RASC, stationed at a town called Hildensheim. It was a shock to my system. Parades, guard duties, booking in and out at the guard room and saluting officers about twenty times a day. It was the complete opposite to what I had been used to. I had decided earlier that I would sign on again when my demob came up but very quickly changed my mind. All the same, although the treatment we received in this camp would have been normal for most units, it was just that the one we had left was so lenient. I got into trouble the first day on Parade. The Sergeant Major inspecting us went round behind me and asked, 'Is that painful?' 'No Sergeant Major.' I said. 'Well, it bloody well should be.' he bellowed. 'I'm standing on your hair. Go and get it cut.'

I didn't know anyone as I had only just been posted there but when I went to our billet that night there was a chap lying on the bed next to mine. As soon as I spoke he knew I was a Scot and asked where I came from. 'Grange, Keith in Banffshire.' I replied. He said, 'I'm from Wick, in Caithness.' He would have been about twelve years older than me and had been in the army for about twelve years. I think his surname was Gunn but I'm not sure. Anyway, one thing led to another and he produced a bottle of Schnapps which we proceeded to demolish. I got talking about my girlfriend back in Wolfenbuttel. 'Has she got a friend?' he asked. 'Yes.' I said. I knew this because Freddy Lunn, one of my mates who came from Liverpool, went with Margaret's friend whom I knew only as Dizzy, and he had been posted back to the UK. 'Right.' He said. 'I'll go and get a truck and we'll go and get the girls.' He told me where to go in the camp and he would pick me up. When he arrived he was driving a ration truck and he had chunks of beef and other foodstuffs stashed away in the cab. This was the truck he normally drove and the loot he had secretly stashed in the cab was for the black market, of course. How he got out of the camp without being challenged I really don't know. Maybe it was because he was so well known by everyone.

Well, we made it to Wolfenbuttel, a distance of about thirty five miles and picked up my girl. Dizzy said she would come by train next day, and she did. Margaret stayed and got lodgings in a house in the town but Dizzy didn't like her date and went home again that night. Gunn managed to put the truck back again and get clear. He was posted a couple of days after that. Just as well, I heard afterwards that he had reached the rank of Sergeant Major which entitled him to his own room. He was demoted down to being just a driver for running a brothel in his room. I also heard that he was in the clink again and that's where I would have been if we had been caught the night I was with him. I was well clear of that gangster. The next scrap I got into came about because of my mate Joe Robb, who lived next to us in Grange. He had worked with me in the forestry before being called up. He was in the Gordon Highlanders and was also stationed in Germany, in Bremenhaven. I got a weekend pass to go and visit him. I went by train as all British

military personnel could travel on trains, buses or trams for free. I had a good time. On the way back, however, there were three Germans in the carriage with me and a fight broke out. One of them was picking his nose and the others got on to him for that. In the disturbance my bonnet was knocked off and went flying out of the window. I had no hope but to go into the camp with no

L to R Dizzy, Freddy Lunn, Margaret Brands

bonnet. Hoping nobody would notice I crept past the Guard Room and thought I was in the clear, but then came a shout, 'SOLDIER, come here.' I was charged with being improperly dressed. Next day I was up in front of the CO, my sentence, three days pay forfeited. That was my doughnut snacks knocked on the head

Photos of some of the squad I served with, myself third from the right

for a couple of days. Every unit in the British Army had a notice board called Standing Orders which was updated at 17.00 hours. Everyone in that unit was supposed to read the notice to find out if his name was posted for any duties the following day. Well, this particular weekend I went out on Saturday and didn't come back until late Sunday evening and forgot to read the standing orders. My name had been up for Guard Duty. I was placed under open arrest and eventually marched up in front of the CO. My sentence, seven days pay forfeited. Another miserable week without doughnuts.

A modification came out for Bedford trucks which was a change in the valve tappet clearance. I spent about ten days doing nothing else but modifying them, not a very nice job. Unlike the 10 Independent Station at Wolfenbuttel we didn't have many German mechanics working with us so we had to do most of the tasks ourselves.

Some of us had to go on a course to Bad Harzburg for three days. Another bloke and I thought we would have a go at skiing as we could draw skis from the store. Well, we put on the skis and got down the slope all right. 'This is OK.' I thought until we reached the bottom and tried to turn round. Of course the skis got all mixed up and I landed on my back. I picked myself up and, of course, we had to walk back up the hill, a mile or so. On reaching the top we quickly put the skis back into the store. I had a very embarrassing experience here. We saw some girls walking about near the camp and I shouted to them in German. We got quite a mouthful in reply, they were English ATS girls out of uniform.

Then the Berlin airlift began and we were posted to Gutersloh Airport where we were staying under canvas two to a tent on camp beds.

I remember it was atrocious weather and the tents were on grass. After a while with so many of us moving about it soon became a sea of mud.

We were there looking after the trucks which were delivering the goods to be transported by plane to Berlin. With a plane taking off and one landing every two minutes it was a busy place with a steady stream of trucks delivering supplies to be flown to Berlin. When we were off duty we could go to the Flight Office and book a flight across to Berlin on one of the planes. We would be assigned to a pilot and he would tell us approximately when to be there. Just two of us to each plane. When the time came we went with the pilots and got on the plane which was a Dakota. I actually went on two trips, the first time they were carrying bags of sugar, about fifteen tons, the second time it was coal. We had to sit on the bags of whatever goods were being transported for take off but after that the pilot would call us through to the cockpit.

I clearly remember passing the border into East Germany, the Russian zone, and there we could see all the guns and tanks massed along the border about three deep. I had never seen so many tanks or guns all in one place before. There was a large column of Russian tanks and other vehicles about two miles back heading towards the border and the pilot radioed in to report this. When we landed in Berlin we were there for about an hour and stayed in the canteen with the pilots until the plane was ready to return. It was a great experience for me to travel there at that time. Another vivid memory I have is of walking back from the cookhouse one day and hearing the sound of an aeroplane but not the usual sound. Suddenly two planes came into view on the grass side by side and then took off. They went into the sky almost vertically. I had never seen a plane take off like that before. They turned out to be jet planes. I had heard about them but this was the first time I had seen them.

Our living quarters, the two man tent, me on the left and John Brown, from Galloway.

In the course of my stay in Germany I learned to speak German. I didn't set out to learn the language but because I had worked alongside so many Germans I just picked it up. The finishing touch came when I dated Margaret Brands. As she couldn't speak much English I spoke to her in German and realized I could manage pretty well. Of course, she helped to polish it up a bit more. I was also able to write it too although Margaret said my spelling was not very good.

I had just come back from road testing this Dodge truck and John Brown said, 'Stand there and get your photo taken.' The lady in the photograph worked in the office and was Egyptian but had been resident in Germany for a good few years.

As I mentioned I had kept in touch with Gerty Short who had worked in the office in Fordyce Lodge while

I worked in the forest there. She was now with the Control Commission in Germany. Although she was a long distance from where I was I don't remember the name of the place. I think it was either in Austria or just on the border with Austria. She wrote to see if I would be interested in a job with the Control Commission as an interpreter. As it was nearly time for my demob I was interested. She put me in touch with the Control Commission office at Sarstedt where I went for an interview. That's when I discovered that the German I had learned was a dialect and I would have to go to school for a couple of months or so to learn proper German. I just hadn't realized that, just as in Britain, different parts of Germany had different dialects. In Britain we learned standard English in school but as soon as the school doors closed we reverted to our local dialect. The same happened in Germany and probably most countries in the world. I had about a month to go to demob and had that time to make up my mind. In the end I decided against it.

Photographs of wrecked German planes scattered about the aerodrome. Note the bullet holes in them

A Civilian Again

After the army I went to the Labour Exchange at Keith and they gave me a card for a job with Bissett Public Works Contractors of Aberdeen, who needed workers for a Hydro Electric scheme they were building at Fannich near Strathpeffer, Ross-shire. My brother, David, was with me, also looking for a job. We reported to the office and the man in charge asked if I could drive. I said 'Yes.' He said they had a vacancy for a chauffeur and would I be interested. I thought this would be a nice easy job so I said 'Yes.' My brother got a job working in the tunnel. I was given this car, a Vauxhall I think, about 18HP. My job was to report to the surveyor's office in the morning and take them wherever they wanted to go. Mostly it was to the tunnel mouth. Sometimes we arrived about 9am, they would disappear and I would not see them again until late in the afternoon. While waiting I just sat and read books, the most boring job I ever had. I only stayed a few weeks and left. My brother left a week later.

I then decided I would like a car so David and I went to the car market in Aberdeen and came home with a 1932 MG two-seater sports model.

Gerty Short on a motorcycle with her friend Jean Charles, from Huntly, who also corresponded with me while I was in the army.

Home on leave from the army with my only means of transport then.

Most cars then were pre 1939 as all car production for the civilian market had been stopped in favour of military requirement.

I went back to the Labour Exchange at Keith. Various jobs were on offer for which I got a couple of cards but then decided to carry on to Dufftown to try some of the distilleries for a job. Coming into the town, I saw a sign for Parkmore Limeworks and thought I would ask if they had any vacancies. They needed a banks man (second man) for a 19RB digger to load the dumpers which transported the rock to the crusher. I also had to learn to drive the digger in case the driver, whose name was McBain, was off sick. It wasn't long before I picked it up. I managed to get a job for David looking after machinery like conveyors and crushers, keeping them greased and maintained.

We stayed in what we called the bothy, an ex-army Nissen hut. One end was filled with bundles of paper bags and our end had beds and a stove in the middle of the floor. It was pretty rough, just the bare corrugated iron sheets. Another occupant of the bothy was Charles Stewart from Glenlivet. By coincidence I had worked with his brother Andrew at Greenhill, Deskford, when I was in the timber trade. There was also a nightwatchman, Sandy McDonald, who spent a lot of his time in the bothy and kept the fire going all night. We took turn about to do the cooking and whoever was on duty got off half an hour early.

After blasting the rock face a lot of the boulders would be too large for the digger, or indeed the crusher, to handle. Because of this, just before noon, we had to put on 'plaster shots'. These consisted of a stick of gelignite with a short fuse, about eighteen inches long. They were placed on top of the boulder and covered with mud or clay. We would have used between fourteen and sixteen shots and three or four of us would have to go round and light the fuses and then take cover. But more than once, while we were lighting the fuses some would go off giving us a hell of a fright. Surprisingly, none of us was ever hurt as the blast always went down and shattered the stone.

David's job, looking after the plant, was no less dangerous. One day he was having difficulty with a conveyor belt slipping on the pulley. The correct procedure would have been to stop the plant and tighten the belt but to save time he decided to apply belt dressing (what we called belt syrup) to the pulley using a short stick when it caught between the pulley and the belt. Before he knew what was happening his arm became trapped between the pulley and the belt. Fortunately, the extra pull on the electric motor tripped the safety switch and there he was, stuck, until the man attending the crusher noticed that the stone was building up on the conveyor. He went to investigate and heard my brother's cries for help. He and a few others managed to wind the belt back and free David's arm. He was rushed to Dufftown Hospital but because his condition was not life threatening I was not told until stopping time. I didn't even stop for supper but went straight to the hospital to find him in quite good spirits. His arm looked terrible, black and blue all over and very painful. He was lucky, he could have lost his arm or even his life. Shortly after that we decided to start up on our own. We bought a Fordson tractor, a plough and also a binder and got work from some of the crofts around Dufftown..

We would plough their fields and cut their crops when ready. There were no combine harvesters around then. I remember ploughing at Netherley, near Auchindoon, and it was snowing. When it started to blow we decided to go home to Grange before the roads filled. The minute we got home our father said, 'Did you let the water out of the tractor for the frost?' Well of course we'd forgotten. We had no hope but to go back, a distance of about twenty four miles and by this time we could only see about two yards in front. We got there, drained the water and set off back home. It was an horrendous journey that took about four hours.

After the snow had melted we went back and finished the ploughing. By this time we were getting short of money so decided to call it a day and give up. Looking back, I realize we could never have succeeded. Having no bank account we worked with cash only, so if the farmer gave us a cheque we had to go to his bank and withdraw the money. We bought the fuel from a garage in Dufftown and took it away in five gallon drums. We kept no books or record of anything.

My brother want home to help my father on the croft. I went back to the labour exchange and got a card for John Laing Public Work Contractors who were rebuilding Milton Aerodrome. I got a job right away on a NCK excavator with a grab attachment, keeping the hoppers at the batching plant topped up. We lived in MOD huts at Calcots and the food from the cookhouse, also MOD, was first class.

By this time I had a Hillman 10hp car and I used to give a couple of men a lift to work. One of the men, George Ross (nicknamed Chiefie) said, 'There is a very nice girl starting here today, my cousin, Doris.' Sure enough there she was dishing out the food. When we had collected ours and sat down at the table I said to Chiefie, 'I wouldn't mind going out with her.' He said, 'No chance, she's spoken for.' I didn't give it another thought, never thinking one day she would be my wife.

This is a tractor similar to the one we had.

Because of the low lying nature of Milton Aerodrome flooding was a constant problem. The water had to be pumped into the River Lossie through a ditch approximately quarter of a mile long, about eight feet deep and sixteen feet wide with steel pilings on both banks. My

This is a binder like the one we owned.

next job was removing and replacing them using a pneumatic hammer fastened to the piling and then to a rope on my digger. I took the strain and the hammer was started up. The horrendous vibration was very

Me loading a lorry.

hard on both machine and driver, just like sitting on top of a cement vibrator. If I was lucky three or four of the pilings were locked together with rust and came out together. Thankfully, hammering the new ones in was easier.

Charles White was in charge of the squad and because he couldn't drive he got me to drive him about with the result I got all the petrol I needed. He also wanted me to teach him to drive but he couldn't make anything of it. On one occasion I took him out and while we were on a long stretch of road a car appeared about half a mile away. He panicked and shouted, 'What'll I do? Put her in nothing? Put her in nothing?' I couldn't help laughing, and that was the end of the driving lessons.

When the work at Milton Airfield was finished we were moved to Lossiemouth Aerodrome which was also to be rebuilt. Again, I was at the batching plant keeping the hoppers topped up. This time we were billeted in wooden huts which Laing had erected for the workmen. The cookhouse had rooms attached for the catering staff, John Ross, the catering manager and three girls, Doris Ross, Gladys Duff and Wendy Fraser. Gordon Ironside, the cook and two older women, Mrs. Bennet and Renee Watson stayed off camp.

One June evening in 1951 I was going in to Elgin to look at another car when Gladys Duff and Wendy Fraser asked for a lift as they were going to the pictures. I said 'Yes, no bother.' So they jumped into the back seat. Just as I was about to move away a head popped round the corner

(left) Doris Ross

(right) My Hilman car with me on the running board.

43

of the building and said, 'Can I come with you?' This, of course, was Doris Ross and I said, 'Yes, jump in.' When we got to Elgin, Gladys and Wendy got off at the Picture House saying they would make their own way home but Doris stayed with me and after I was finished my business we went back to the camp. I asked her if she would go out with me the next night, she said, 'Yes.' and we went out together every night after that. The very next weekend she went home to Cromdale and finished with her former boyfriend.

John Ross the catering manager was her uncle and that's how she got the job at Lossiemouth. Before that she had worked in the co-operative shop in Grantown on Spey learning to be a baker. Unfortunately she contracted pneumonia and pleurisy, by all accounts she was pretty bad and at one time it was touch and go as to whether she would survive. An x-ray revealed a shadow on her lungs which they thought might be tuberculosis. She was told that it was not advisable to work in the bakery any longer because of the flour dust and to try to get a job near the sea. It turned out that it was not TB and in later life another x-ray confirmed the shadow was still there suggesting she had been born with it.

Doris Ross with her pal Gladys Duff.

Doris Ross with the huts in the background.

Another story about Doris comes to mind concerning one of the men who worked on the site. He had a reputation for grabbing the girls and Doris was not having any of it. She set out to fix him and fix him she did. One of her jobs was to go across to a hanger about half a mile from the cookhouse and set the dining tables ready for the managers, gaffers and engineers by noon. This individual was a van driver, a gopher (go for this and go for that). One of his main jobs was to be at the cookhouse for 11am to load up with the containers of food and tea urns and transport them to the hanger. Doris was supposed to go with him but she preferred to walk. As part of her plan to 'fix' the troublemaker she grew her nails long, pointed them with a nail file and waited her chance. On this particular day the gopher had a puncture on his van at the cookhouse. A mechanic was called from the workshop to change the wheel. A forklift driver, David MacLeod, was working nearby and the mechanic asked him to lift the van to save using the jack, so David saw all the commotion that followed. It was a warm summer day and the gopher had on a short sleeved shirt. Sure enough he caught hold of Doris when she was loading the van. As quick as a flash Doris caught hold of one of his arms with both hands and dug her nails in with all her strength. Of course he tried to pull away - the worst thing he could have done. He had six or seven deep wounds on his arm and there was blood everywhere. 'Now you bastard.' she said, 'Go home and tell your wife what you got that for!' His wounds turned septic and he was off his work for a week. I will always remember David McLeod's comment when he was telling us what happened. 'What a tiger that Doris Ross is. We had better keep clear of her.' Well, as you know I didn't take his advice and never regretted that. The gopher never spoke to Doris again so she accomplished what she had set out to do. After I started dating her I said 'I think you put poison on your nails and that is why his arm festered.' She replied, 'No, I never thought of that or I would have.'

We'd been going out together for a couple of months when another alarming episode took place, this time at night. In the layout of the living quarters there was a passage with rooms along both sides. The other two girls had rooms on the left of the passage and Doris had a room to herself on the opposite side. Further along were rooms for two engineers and also her uncle's room. Doris suddenly woke up this night and as she described it to me, she saw this face looking down on her with two teeth sticking out like a walrus. 'Get out of my room.' she shouted. Her uncle hearing the commotion, came and took the man, an Irishman, away. A crowd of them had all been out drinking including her uncle. Doris's starting time was five a.m. as she had to get everything ready for the breakfast at seven a.m. When I went in for breakfast I knew something was up. She told me the whole story and what a temper she was in. She was just waiting for her uncle to appear and she was going to tell him that she was leaving. She did this and said she would tell her father all about the drinking sessions her uncle was having. No way would she stay in a place where she was not safe in her bed. I said I would run her home with all her stuff in the evening.

She went to her room to pack and wait for me. Shortly afterwards her uncle appeared and said that if he gave her a room round the back to herself would she stay. This room had been an office at one time, it was still attached to the cook house but had just one door to the outside. She agreed to stay but only because she didn't want to be parted from me. It was the best thing that ever happened. Instead of courting in the car as before we now had a room to do our courting in.

When the batching was finished I was moved back to Charlie White's squad. Apparently he had asked for me specially. I was back among pilings again but they were very different from the steel pilings. These were reinforced concrete with a steel tip, 75 feet long by 3 feet square. I had a 110 foot crane jib fitted and my job was to lift these concrete pilings into a wooden framework which held them plumb. A steel hat was placed over the top of the piling with a block of wood between the piling and the hat which helped to absorb the hammering. This had to be changed every second piling. I then had to lift up a steam hammer which was fixed on to the top of the hat and as the piling was hammered I had to keep the rope just slightly slack. These pilings were the foundation for the Control Tower and were hammered in until they hit rock. Most of them stopped at a depth of between 40 and 50 feet but some went down as far as 64 feet.

As this was a rush job we got a lot of overtime and we also got a bonus, nothing for the first piling but 10s. for every one after that. We never managed more than three a day but twice I had over £30.00 for my week's work, a very good wage when you consider that the average labourer's pay packet was about £9.00 for the week. As machine drivers our average wage was about £14.00 per week. In all I think about two hundred pilings had to be hammered in.

Shortly after I started courting Doris she asked me to go home with her to meet her parents Bill and Mary Ross. They lived in a railway house at Cromdale where her father worked with British Rail. That was a real eye opener for me as her upbringing had been completely different from mine. She could speak to her parents on any subject, everything was discussed openly in her family. I could never have spoken to my parents about the things Doris discussed with her folk. But I believe it was the right way and all my children were brought up to discuss all kinds of things openly with us and my grandchildren seem to be having the same sort of upbringing.

Her mother was a very fine person and I liked her very much. I really liked her father as well but he was a character! His nickname was the Cromdale Poacher. He worked with British Rail as a ganger on the Permanent Way. That was his day job, his night job was poaching. He

This is the machine with the 110ft jib.

This was Charlie White's squad. I can't remember their names but Charlie White is in the middle in shirt sleeves sixth from the right. I am second right in a boiler suit. In the background is the wooden frame work for holding the pilings plumb.

also had a large garden full of vegetables in the growing season. All the years after we got married until they moved to a council flat in Grantown on Spey we came home laden with fresh vegetables after every visit to their home in Cromdale. Sometimes he gave us a pheasant, a cut of salmon perhaps and sometimes part of a deer. But it didn't stop there. Once when we had gone up there for the weekend he asked me on the Saturday night if I would like to accompany him on what he called the 'hooch run'. 'Yes.' I said. Later on two of his neighbours appeared to take part. The Balmenach Distillery, just up the road from their house, had a steam railway engine to haul wagons loaded with barrels of whisky down to Cromdale Station where they would be collected by British Rail and delivered to their destination. Back then all the railway wagons were made with wood bolted on to an iron frame. This was the ploy. Armed with a long auger for drilling wood the men would crawl underneath the wagon after a rough measurement to find where the barrels were situated. A hole was drilled up through the wooden wagon floor right in to the barrel of whisky. They had a pail ready into which they caught the whisky. When they had enough they 'chapped' a prepared stick up into the hole in the barrel to seal it and then broke it off. They crawled out again and the whisky was shared out among them.

Bill Ross

Mary Ross

This is the Balmenach Puggie that pulled the whisky loaded wagons to Cromdale Station.

Sometime in August 1951 Doris and I got engaged. We went to Aberdeen where I bought her an engagement ring and we called in past my parents house to give them the news. They were really surprised. After we left there we headed back to the camp at Lossiemouth. On the way I decided I would go for a dram in Keith to celebrate. Doris wouldn't go into a pub so I took a couple of drams out to her and off we set again. Fochabers was the next stop and I visited a pub there. Doris still wouldn't come in so I took drams out to her again. Then we set off for Lossiemouth, not to the camp but to the Steamboat Bar where I met a few of our workmates and told them I had just got engaged. Bad move. Drinks were coming from all directions and Doris was still sitting in the car outside with the engine still running because the battery wasn't very good. If I had stopped the car I would have had to use the crank to start it again. Doris was getting pretty merry by this time and across the road, sitting on a wall were three or four old fishermen. Well, with the car engine still running it was belching out a fair bit of smoke which was blowing across the road into their faces. They started arguing with Doris and of course with her having had a few drams she was arguing back. The upshot of this was that someone sent for the police. Somebody came into the pub and told me what was going on outside. I went out with Joe Mitchell who also worked with Laing. By now the police were questioning me but I was so drunk all I could see was two blue blurs. They didn't charge me and Joe said he would drive me to the camp (even though he didn't have a licence). The police said that was a good idea but that I would have to go to the Police Station the next day to show them my driving licence and insurance certificate. When I went into the Police Station I found it was the same two officers that had been on duty the night before. One of them said, 'We didn't think you were all that bad and you did have something to celebrate.'

We had a bit of a blether and I discovered that they both came from Macduff and had been in Lossiemouth on relief. As I was brought up in Grange I was very broad-spoken, just as they were, I think that helped greatly. That was the first and only time that I have ever been drunk while driving. I learned a lesson that day I can tell you.

My next job was with a drag line attachment. To the north of the aerodrome was an old road which had linked Lossiemouth to Hopeman and Burghead. It was now absorbed into the grounds of the aerodrome and a new road had been built for civilian traffic. The old road was two or three feet higher than the rest of the area and my job was to bring it down to ground level. When I started digging I came upon three copper electric cables, one of them as thick as your arm. I always kept an axe in the excavator as quite often we found copper cables. I would tear out lengths and as I was loading the trucks the drivers cut the cables into shorter lengths. There were two trucks to take the rubble away. One man was an owner driver from Fochabers who offered to collect the cables and sell it to a scrap merchant. In the end, however, he double crossed us and never shared the money he got for the cable with us.

By this time I was teaching Doris to drive and she was getting on really well. We used my old Hillman for her lessons. Apart from the brakes being nearly non existent there were other problems. If you turned the steering wheel too far to the left the steering would lock and you had to stop and reverse until it freed itself. Men were in the process of putting up a gate at the entrance to the camp, one with a single bar and a counter weight which lifted up. They had just cemented in the timber posts at each side which had been left for the cement to cure. Well, we were coming back to the camp with Doris driving and as she turned to go through the gate she turned the steering wheel too far to the left and as a result the steering locked and the car kept turning and hit the left post breaking it off at ground level. This was in the evening, nobody saw it happen so we kept going into the camp. Because we hit the post with the centre of the bumper there wasn't a mark on the car so we got away with it.

We had now set the date for our wedding which was to be the 11th of January, 1952. We tried to buy a caravan but found them to be away above our price range. Someone told me about an old bus which belonged to a man by the name of Ritchie, from Rafford near Forres, so we went to see it. He had started to convert it into a home but his circumstances changed and he no longer had a use for it. We bought it quite cheaply and I set about making it into a home for us.

Some time about November something happened which I regret to this day. Working with Laing and staying in the camp was a man (we'll call him George Craig). I had been at school with him and he approached me one day and asked if I would lend him my car as he had two truck wheels to take into Elgin. His car was a Ford 8 but only had two doors and he couldn't get the wheels in. Also in the picture was an Irishman called John Gallacher and as he was a bit of a 'boozer' I wasn't too happy about him and George Craig using my car. 'No, sorry,' I said, 'but I will run you into Elgin if you like.' George Craig's father was a blacksmith who built tractor trailers and also bought and sold wheels and tyres as part of his business. I assumed that was where they had come from. If I had only asked myself how he got the wheels into the camp in the first place if they wouldn't go into his car - but I didn't. I took them to Elgin where they went to a haulage contractor and that was when I began to have serious doubts about them while listening to the three of them in conversation. True to form as soon as they were paid the Irishman said, 'Come on to the pub and we'll have a dram.' I refused and said that if they went to the pub I was not going to wait for them. The Irishman went off on his own. On the way home to the camp George admitted that they had stolen the wheels, one off either side of a British Road Services truck which was parked at the side of one of the huts at the camp. The driver went home every night to Buckie in the workers' bus. He just jumped into his lorry in the morning and set off for Inverness to pick up some stuff. He was approaching Nairn when he heard a clunking noise and stopped to investigate. That's when he found two of his wheels were missing. The clunking was caused by Craig and Gallacher who hadn't bothered to tighten the nuts properly. The police were called of course and it wasn't long before they collared Craig and Gallacher. It was the weekend and I was home at Grange. On the Sunday two policemen came and charged me. They were going to arrest me and take me to Elgin Police Station. I asked if I could take my car and hand myself in. They agreed to this. When I got there I was locked in a cell and on Monday morning we were up in court. We were allocated a solicitor and when I told him the story he advised me to plead guilty, which I did. The first to be sentenced was Gallacher who was jailed for six months. Craig was jailed for three months. By this time I was really worried but I just got fined £12.00. Of course what I didn't know was that the pair had stolen a lot more stuff including heavy duty batteries off some of the machines. My biggest disappointment was that I lost my job which I had really liked. Before my involvement with the two criminals I had been asked if I was prepared to become a permanent member of staff and move with the firm to wherever they had work. I had agreed because they were a cracker of a firm to work with. Perhaps, though, things turned out for the best.

My next job was driving a lorry for a game dealer from Cromdale. This was only for a few weeks over Christmas but I can say without doubt that it was the worst job I ever had. Two of us had to load four hundred hares and other game and deliver them to Smithfield Market in London before 9am on Monday but we couldn't get away before mid-day on the Sunday as we had to wait until all the poachers who had been busy on the Saturday had checked their snares on the Sunday morning. The lorry was a Ford Thames V8 with a petrol engine with very poor brakes, cable operated and with no power assistance. Back then there were no motorways so we couldn't waste time if we were to reach London before 9am. When we reached Smithfield the hares at the bottom of the load were all as flat as a sheet of paper and stinking.

On one trip we had to call at a place just outside Shrewsbury to collect a car and its owner, a gamekeeper from Grantown on Spey, who had arranged to get a lift home with us. We loaded the car on the back of the lorry and secured it with ropes. As there was no room in the cab of the lorry the gamekeeper had to sit in his car during the journey. I was driving at the time and as we passed through Shrewsbury a woman jumped out in front of the lorry. How I missed her I don't really know as there was no chance of the brakes stopping us. As it was a one way street, there was no traffic coming towards us and somehow I managed to swing out past her and stopped to see if she was all right. Suddenly two policemen appeared and helped her to her feet. They told me not to worry as this was not the first time it had happened. Too much alcohol was the problem I think. I got quite a fright but the gamekeeper got a bigger one. With me swerving so fast a rope had snapped, the car had lurched across and was teetering on the edge of the platform. We had to rectify that and then carried on home with no more mishaps.

As I was only taken on for Christmas and New Year, the job lasted three and a half weeks during which time I did the London run three times. I was paid off on January 5th and that worked out just fine as our wedding was arranged for January 11th.

We were married in the manse at Cromdale. I had wanted to be married in the registry office while Doris wanted a church wedding. We compromised and the minister married us in the manse, just Doris and her bridesmaid and me with David, my best man. The reception was held at Doris's parents' house in Cromdale where we were joined by my mother and father and a few friends. In the morning we went by train to Inverness, where my aunt lived, for our honeymoon. If we hadn't bought a return ticket we would have had to walk home as we had no more money and I didn't even have a job to go to. The bus was ready to move in to, though, and it was parked at my father's croft at Grange.

After we got settled in I went job hunting. I worked a short time at Blackhillock Limeworks, in Keith, driving a tractor spreading lime. Soon after that I found a better job at Parkmore Limeworks, in Dufftown, driving an ex-army Chevrolet truck with a lime spreader fitted on the back. It was very hard work. Two of us were sent out to farms, usually in Aberdeenshire, with a load of lime. After that load had been spread we had to go to the nearest railway station to meet railway wagons full of lime. We had to hand shovel the hard packed lime on to the spreader. Every shovel full had to be stamped out just as you would when digging the garden. We got a bonus of one penny per ton which meant we could make up to £1.10s extra per week. Considering the average weekly wage was about £10.00 per week it was a great help.

By this time we had moved the bus to Dufftown. A chap I knew called Bremner had a small garage in Aberchirder and he had trade plates so he moved it for me. I was going to drive it myself without trade plates or a road licence but my wife wouldn't hear of it. Just as well, as the police appeared to see if it was licensed and, if not, how had it been moved. Apparently someone had reported that it was not licensed.

I had changed my car again and now had an Austin Seven. My wife was still learning to drive and one time, on our way to Grange to visit my folks, we fell out about something. She stopped the car, jumped out and said that she was never going to drive again. I had no option but to go into the driving seat and take over. Further down the road a bit was Berrilies Brae which was not very steep. This Austin had a hand throttle on the steering wheel. I put the car in a low gear, set the hand throttle then jumped out so Doris had no option but to get into the driving seat. Well, she didn't half get her own back. She just kept going slowly and when I reached the car she would speed up again. In the end I just sat down at the road side and she eventually came back for me. It fixed the disagreement though.

This is the Austin Seven, universally known as the 'Puddle Jumper' with Doris in front.

Doris and myself.

The job at Parkmore was not working out well for us. I would leave at about 7am and not get back until 9pm, completely exhausted and ready for bed. It was a very lonely life for my wife, although she never complained. I hadn't been there long when I fell out with the mechanic who looked after the transport. The company had about eight spreaders in use and every day we would be assigned a spreader, not always the same one. One day, when I started up my spreader I could hear it was knocking. I informed the mechanic whose answer was, 'I am the person to say when an engine is knocking - get going with it.' I had a bit of an argument with him but did as I was told and set off. Well, I just got into the field when there was a bang and the connecting rod came through the side of the engine block. I was then towed home to the garage where I had another go at the mechanic - a big mistake. I don't know what he told the manager but he couldn't even wait until the next day. He came over to the bus and sacked me. It turned out well though, I got a far better job. The next day I went to Newmill of Keith where my uncle worked for a building firm called Robert Paterson

Building Contractors Ltd. He had told me there was a vacancy for a lorry driver. I went to the office and was told to come in. There was Mr. Paterson with his telephone all in pieces. He said, 'I am trying to repair this damned phone.' and kept working on it whilst asking me questions. I was honest with him about how I got the sack. 'I'm not that bothered. I like to find out for myself, so when can you start?' I said, 'Tomorrow.' and he said, 'Capital.' and I must say that Bertie, as he was affectionately known by everyone, was the best boss I had ever worked for. He also had a concrete block factory at Kingston on Spey and that was where I worked from, driving blocks to various building projects across the north east.

The lorry I had was a flat bed ex-army seven ton petrol Austin, although most of the time we were carrying at least ten tons. Bertie also bought redundant MOD huts and I would sometimes have to go and take loads of hut sections and Nissen huts home to his yard. He sold a lot of them to farmers. He also had two ex-army Austin six wheelers and a Leyland Beaver pulling a trailer. The Leyland had a steady job driving foam slag from the iron works in Glasgow to be used to make lightweight blocks. The driver was Robert Roy with Charles Christie as second man. Back then you had to have a second man if you were pulling a trailer.

By this time we had moved the bus down to a site at Auchinhove farm about a mile and a half from Keith on the Banff road. The road had been realigned and we were on part of the old road. We got permission to stay there from the farmer, Mr. Hendry. He also allowed us to collect our water from the farm. The year was 1953 and the gales in January created havoc round the country flattening acres of trees. One morning my lorry wouldn't start because of the wind and rain so I walked to the yard at Newmill, about a mile and a quarter. A few of the men were trying to save the garage roof which was in danger of blowing off. We managed to secure the roof but the wind was getting worse and Bertie said we might as well all go home. One of the other drivers gave me a lift and I got home to find my wife, who was about seven months pregnant, sitting out in the lorry cab because the wind was so bad she thought the bus was going to tip over. We had a small wood burning stove and there was a small amount of petrol in the bus tank so it could have been very dangerous. She was absolutely frozen stiff so I got the other driver to give us a pull to start my truck and we went to my father's croft so she could get warmed up. I was worried about her and the baby's health but everything turned out fine. On the 26th of February, 1953, in Keith hospital, my daughter Jane was born. I didn't find out until I came home from work and there was a note left to say she was in hospital. Dr. Taylor had been passing and he decided to take her in. Only a week earlier he had seen her struggling up from the farm carrying two pails of water and had stopped to give her a telling off saying if he saw her doing that again he would 'skelp her backside'.

The day after my daughter was born I was in a hurry to get home as I was late and wanted to visit the hospital. I had been pushing the truck as fast as I could and when I stopped at the office it kept running for a few moments because the pre-ignition was on. Bertie said, 'You must have been thrashing that motor.' I admitted that I had and told him the reason. His reply was, 'So what are you standing there for? Get going and we'll sort out your paperwork in the morning.'

Not long after this, I was finishing my supper when a lorry stopped outside and I heard the horn blow. I went out to see what they wanted and here was Bertie driving a six wheel Leyland Hippo. He shouted, 'Aren't you coming to see your new lorry?' To give you an idea of what kind of machine it was, it had actually been new in 1934 and was bought off the showmen when they were finished with it. Bertie had put it through his workshop and although Leslie Finnie, the mechanic, had done any necessary repairs, there is only so much you can do with a twenty year old lorry. Bertie asked me if I would move to Garmouth where the block factory was based as most of my loads out would originate from there and that's how we landed in Garmouth.

When Doris was carrying our second child she was doing a bit of painting close to the time the baby was due. By the time I arrived home from work she was having labour pains and decided it was time to go to the hospital in Buckie. First we had to clean all the paint off her hands. She had also managed to get some on her feet and as she couldn't reach them I had to wash them. I had great difficulty getting the paint off and eventually got some petrol to clean them while she did the same with her hands. At last, with the pains coming closer, we got going.

We had just passed Fochabers when she asked me to stop for a minute because the bumping of the car was making her want to give birth. This happened about five times but we finally arrived at the hospital and within five minutes our son, John, was born. I was very glad to see the hospital. This was on the 27th of July, 1954.

I went to see her every night. One day when I went to work I forgot to put the cat out. By the time I got home the poor cat had been desperate and while trying to get out one of the windows had made a mess on my one and only dress shirt hanging below the window. I had no hope but to wash it and as I didn't have time to dry it I just put it on wet. Damned uncomfortable. Doris didn't half laugh about that. By the time I got home my shirt was dry.

My second daughter Ann was born at Buckie on the 22nd of May, 1955 and then my second son William was born on the 12th of March,1956. My third daughter, Brenda, was a late one being born at Buckie on the 11th of April, 1964.

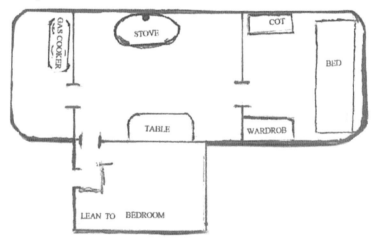

This drawing shows the layout of the old bus with the lean to, which I built on at Blinkbonnie, where Jane, John and Ann slept. William slept in the cot. By the time we moved into our first house, which we built ourselves, we had lived in the bus for ten years. Jane was then nine years old, John seven, Ann was six and William was five.

This is the bus that we stayed in for ten years with the block factory at Kingston in the background.

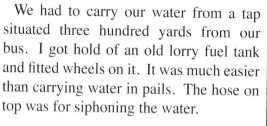

We had to carry our water from a tap situated three hundred yards from our bus. I got hold of an old lorry fuel tank and fitted wheels on it. It was much easier than carrying water in pails. The hose on top was for siphoning the water.

Doris and Jane.

The Water Tank

I think I should mention that we did have two arm chairs in the bus. They consisted of two bucket seats from an old car which I modified and fitted with legs and I must say they were very comfortable. Another good thing about living in the bus was that we had no council tax to pay nor did we have to pay for water or rates.

Shortly after we moved out of the bus a chap by the name of Victor Burnett was in need of somewhere to stay after falling out with his brother, Hector. The two bachelors had lived on a farm and when his brother threw him out Victor had nowhere to go. I offered him the old bus and he jumped at the chance. In fact he lived there for about six years. I didn't charge anything for it but he was very good to my children. They were not always so good to him though. There was a small shed beside the bus where he used to keep coal and firewood and one day, when he went into the shed, some of my children shut the door and locked it. They then found a bee smoker and set it smoking under the door. He was coughing, swearing and shouting what he was going to do to them when he got out. When he finally did get out they hid in a caravan lying in the yard. Victor went in to find them but they climbed out of a window and locked him in again. They were on their way to find the bee smoker again when my wife stopped them and they let him out. Luckily he saw the funny side of it.

He worked as a sawmiller at a yard in Forres. He liked a good drink, especially at weekends. My wife used to take the key out of his Austin Mini if she knew he had been drinking. Once he had a bit more than usual and came to the house window asking for the key. My wife refused and he said, 'Yer a richt fine quine, gie ma the keys for ma Meenie.' My wife said 'No.' 'Ach, Doris, gie me the key, yer an awfy fine quine.' Doris again said, 'No, you have had far too much to drink.' No longer a fine quine, he called her for, 'a the coorse buggers that ever lived.'

This happened more than once and we had a great laugh at his expense. He was such a great character when he was sober. We were sad when he became ill and died. The bus was in such a state of filth and stank so badly I set fire to it. That was the end of our first home.

As well as making concrete blocks Paterson also manufactured precast stuff such as lintels and windowsills. They also made trevises which were used as dividers between stalls in byres. Cattle troughs were cast to be put into the fields by farmers and connected to the water supply. The troughs weighed about twelve hundredweights each. A plumber in Wick had a contract to be supplied with troughs and every so often we had to deliver a load of about twenty. Back then it was a two day job, one day to get to Wick, bed and breakfast and home the next day. At least it was easy to unload them there as the plumber had a forklift. If I was delivering, troughs and trevises to farmers I carried a selection of rollers, crowbars and a couple of old tyres. I had to lift up one end of the trough with a crowbar and slip in a roller, which was just an off cut from a steel tube, then roll it to the side of the lorry, put a couple of tyres down and tip the trough on to the tyres. Sometimes, if they were handy, I would use square straw bales. We had to do the same thing with the trevises. They were more easily broken so we had to be a bit more careful with them. The lintels and window sills usually went to building sites with plenty of men to manhandle them off.

The old Leyland was a desperate machine. When going slowly up a brae I had to stick my head out of the window, which was easy as there was no glass in it, because there was more smoke inside the cab than was coming out of the exhaust. Another time I remember I was going to Banff with a load of concrete blocks. The engine was not performing as it should have been and going up through Cullen, which has quite a steep brae, I could only get as far as the square when the engine would die on me. I phoned the office and Bertie answered. He said, 'Weel ma loon, take off half your load, dump them on the square, deliver the half in the lorry then come back for the rest.' And that was what I had to do. I don't think I would have stayed with any other firm but Bertie was such a good boss I couldn't fall out with him and I really liked the job. The transport, though, was just scrap. Leslie Finnie was head mechanic and did well to keep them all running. A pet saying of his about some of his repairs was, 'Rough but effective.' And he was rough. One episode I will always remember was when a chap from Fochabers, Kenny Gray, had his lorry in for repairs, a problem with fuel. Kenny was sent out to one of the building sites in a van with some of the workmen while the truck was being repaired. I had been sent there with a load of blocks. Kenny asked me if there was any word of his truck being repaired and I said, 'Yes.' Kenny asked what Leslie Finnie had done to it and I said that he had bypassed all the fuel pumps and had fitted a fifty gallon drum on to the roof of the cab. The foreman on the job, Henry Davidson, who was a joiner, quick as a flash said, 'Oh yes, I drilled the holes on the roof for the straps to hold the drum.' Kenny, of course, believed me and started calling Finnie all the derogatory names he could think of and that no way would he drive a lorry with the diesel tank on the roof of the cab. Everybody seeing him on the road would be laughing at him and he was leaving that very day. Although it wasn't true, I'm sure if it had been the best way to repair the lorry and keep it running Leslie Finnie would have done just that.

Henry Davidson, the foreman I mentioned, was another character always up to some caper. I remember going down to a farm at Old Rayne where they were putting up a Dutch barn. These were built with steel uprights and a roof, no sides. It was a day of pouring rain and when I arrived four men were up on the roof absolutely soaked. I said, 'What's wrong with them, have they all gone mad?' He said that they had been giving him harassment so when the rain came on he removed the ladder. 'That'll larn them.' He then had to put the ladder back because they had to unload my lorry.

In the spring, Moray County Council started to stock pile chips in various lay-bys across Moray. This was for chipping the roads in the summer and that created a big demand for lorries. Most of the chips came from Kingston on Spey where a firm by the name of Geddes had a crusher down on the beach and I thought this would be a chance to get a lorry of my own on the road. I approached them and they said, 'You get a lorry and we will give you work.' I knew of an Austin seven ton tipper which belonged to a friend of mine. I bought it as he had replaced it with a better one on the condition that I paid him when I got paid for the work.

In those days there were four kinds of licences, an 'A licence' which allowed you to drive most types of goods for anyone, anywhere. A 'B licence', which was very restricted, naming the materials you were allowed to drive and a certain radius from your operating base. The 'C licence' covered your own goods only and an 'A Contract', which allowed you to drive only for a named firm with whom you had a signed contract. This was the one I should have had and Geddes said they would give me a signed contract. In fact they never did. I drove road chippings for them for about three months without a licence. When the rush was over they paid me off anyway. I managed to pay for the lorry with a bit to spare and I also had the truck to sell. I didn't leave my job, I got my brother David to drive the truck for me. We were very lucky to avoid being stopped by the police. I don't think Geddes ever intended giving me a contract and that was my second failed attempt at my own business.

Shortly after I got talking with a chap called Tommy Rowe who also worked at the block factory. He told me that he had a brother in the south of England, in the London area with, I think, a van from which he went out and sold fruit and vegetables. He appeared to be doing quite well and he suggested that we might have a go and that he would show me the ropes. I traded in my car for a five cwt. Ford van with the intention of having a go at this in our two weeks holiday period. We actually did quite well so I decided to leave my job.

I got my fruit supplies from a wholesale firm called Harrison and Reeves of Elgin. As I got to know the workers they were pretty good to me with special offers and giving me extra weight. I got the vegetables from Springfield Market Gardens in New Elgin, now a housing scheme.

The van I had bought was a bit of a disaster. The worst problem with it was starting it first thing in the morning. I eventually fixed it though. I got a blow lamp and heated the manifold, which was a bit of a nuisance, but it worked. I then decided I would buy a better van and saw one advertised in Kintore, an Austin high top which I bought. It gave me room to carry more goods. I did manage to eke out a living in this business but it was pretty poor and I didn't like the job that much. One of my customers was a firewood merchant, Jock Mackintosh. He had his yard about half a mile south of Garmouth and was looking for a part time worker for three days a week. I decided to go out with the van on three days, picking my best rounds and working with Jock the other three days. This worked quite well and after a few weeks he asked if I would go into partnership with him and stop the fruit and veg. I said, 'Yes.' A big mistake. The first two weeks we made a living wage, but only just. To try and help matters I decided we would run our lorry, a

Receipt for vegetables.

Receipt for fruit.

This was the Ford Van.

The Austin High Top Van.

petrol Leyland Cub, on paraffin (kerosene) which was less than half the price of petrol. To start it I had to pour some petrol from a bottle into the manifold, press the starter and keep full throttle on for about thirty seconds. This worked well as long as I was pulling a load to keep the heat up. Trouble would happen when on a side road, without a load and going slow, the engine would cool and stop. I lived at the end of a rough road with whin bushes on both sides and, one day, the engine started misfiring. I knew it was getting cold so I grabbed the bottle to pour some petrol into the manifold. As I poured, the engine backfired through the manifold and set the bottle alight. I threw it out of the open window but by this time the whole cab was in flames. I knocked the lorry our of gear and followed the bottle out of the cab and landed amongst the whin and bramble bushes. I was picking thorns from all over my body for weeks. The fire in the cab was just a flash which went out so the only damage was to me, the driver.

Every Saturday we split the profit and that was our wages. By the fourth Saturday Jock counted the profit and handed me £2/10s for the week which was no use to anyone. I still had the Austin van and proceeded to take the van body off and build on a platform. The van licence had run out by this time and I had no money to renew it, but nearby lay acres of scrub land with a lot of feral trees. I armed myself with a hacksaw and proceeded to cut down a few of the smaller ones, trailed them home, cut them into blocks, bagged them and sold them locally to make enough money to renew the licence. Meanwhile, my wife was good friends with a couple in Cromdale. Sandy Watt owned a sawmill so Doris contacted them and asked if we could buy a load of fire wood and pay for it after we had cut and sold it. His answer was, 'Yes.' So off we went for a load. After loading up I asked him how much I owed him. His answer was, 'This load is for free just to get you started.' This really made my day and I was so grateful. About four miles from home one of my front tyres burst so I put on the spare but after about another mile it burst as well. Luckily, a friend, Jackie Anderson, also a firewood merchant from Kingston, came along and said that he had a couple of spare wheels and tyres and he would go and fetch one for me to borrow until I got sorted out. Of course all the trouble was caused by having so much weight on the lorry. Eventually I managed to get a couple of second hand tyres and returned the borrowed one.

I had an engine driven circular saw which I got from Jock Mackintosh so I was on my way at last and started to make some money. I decided I needed a bigger lorry so I bought a seven ton petrol driven Albion

The Albion

A Case tractor similar to the one I used to drive my running saw bench.

FT3. Ian Anderson, who lived next door, needed a job so I employed him. One of my suppliers was a Mrs. Bremner with a sawmill in Forres where I could load as many slabs as I could manage for £1/00.

By now I was selling over eight hundred bags a week, over half of them bagged by my wife, on her own, while I was out delivering. The bags we used were bought from a wholesale firm in Elgin, Gordon and MacPhail. They bought sugar in hundredweight bags and repackaged it into 2lb paper bags. We would saw up slabs of wood, anything three inches thick or over went into a separate pile and they were sold as logs for which we charged 2/- per bag for fir, 2/6 for hardwood and the slabs were 1/6. I then hit on an idea to cut the price of the bags of slabs. At that time the farmers took delivery of bags of nitro chalk which they spread on the farm. I asked them to keep the empty bags for me and I used them for the slabs. They held approximately a quarter less than the sugar bags and I sold them for one shilling a bag. Everyone thought they were getting a real bargain. As a result my sales doubled so I had to employ another man, my brother Gordon. As well as selling the firewood in bags I also sold blocks per load but that was mostly hard wood. I had also picked up a running bench so I could cut round logs into boards and posts.

Per Bag Fir Blocks 2/- (10p)
Hardwood Blocks 2/6 (12½p)
Fir Slabs 1/- (5p)

I had this good going business but never kept any records. I just paid the men from the takings. It never entered my head that I should keep records. Eventually the tax man caught up with me and demanded £500.00. Well, there was no way could I afford to pay that. I was telling the local butcher George Henderson when he came round with his van and he gave me the address of his accountant in Elgin, Harry Clark. I went to see him and he fixed it for me in the end. I didn't have to pay anything and, of course, I took on my two employees officially.

We were still staying in the converted bus with the four children. From left, William, Ann, John and Jane.

William, myself and Jane with Ann in front. In the background some slabs waiting to be cut.

63

He also showed my wife how to do the books, including keeping a record of our employees earnings. The firewood business wasn't an easy job. I was working about fourteen hours a day, Saturday and Sunday, no holidays, and my wife working with me as well as looking after the four children, but it was quite a profitable business. left is a newspaper cutting dated 20/3/1958 when I was warned for not having a near side mirror and fined £2.00 for not keeping records of my driving hours. I didn't even have a record book.

Doris filling bags of firewood

About this time I got the chance to buy the land where my yard and bus were situated. The owner was Mr. George Reid and I bought the eight acres altogether for which I paid £20.00. I was quite proud because I was now a landowner. About the same time, I was in Elgin with a load of wood where I had a very good round in the Bishopmill area. After I had sold all the bags I went to the chip shop for a fish supper. Back then the chips were always wrapped in old newspapers and as I was eating the fish and chips I read the paper. I saw an advert from the Capital Lime Co. asking for people to deliver and spread lime. I applied and got word back within a week to go to Aberdeen for an interview at the St. George's Hotel. The deal was that they would supply us with a lime spreader and keep so much off our monthly account to pay for it. Within a week I got word I had the job. That is when I took my brother Gordon, employed by me in the firewood business and my brother David, who supplied the tractor to pull the spreader into the business and Baillie Brothers came into being. We had to buy another lorry and on my rounds I had seen an

Albion FT3, the same as the one we already had, lying derelict at the Star Garage in Buckie and at a price we could afford, so we went to have a look at it.

My brother, David Baillie's, David Brown tractor which now belonged to Baillie Brothers.

My father, David Baillie Senior, driving a 1923 Fordson. A neighbour, Adam McWilliam standing on the bogie.

The first thing we noticed was that it had no windscreen. The garage man assured us that it was in running order when it had arrived there. He went and got a battery, pressed the button and it started. It seemed fairly sound so, after a wee bit of haggling, I got it for £20.00. We took it home and set about fitting a windscreen. We didn't have a proper one but found a screen that wasn't far off the size and with a bit of fiddling and hacking we managed to fit it. Of course, in those days there was no MOT (just as well) so we got it licensed and started carting lime.

This was an 'A Contract', as I mentioned earlier, where we were only supposed to carry goods for the Capital Lime Co. not even goods for ourselves. In fact we did, but not often. We did get warned once, someone had reported us.

The lime came by boat to Burghead Harbour. Frances Stewart drove the crane fitted with a grab and unloaded the boats. The lime was stored on the pier and then loaded on to the trucks. There were two other contractors who started at the same time. One was Wattie Dey, from Alves. He had a Dodge diesel truck which was a lot better than our two Albions. The other was Edward Kaminski from Forres. He was Polish and had an old petrol Bedford. He was a kind of a make do and mend merchant like ourselves. He sometimes had his son John, who was still at school, along with him. He would buy chewing gum for his son and would say, 'Johnnie, no spit out, no swallow. I need for radiator.' The gum was to patch pinholes in the radiator. Apparently it worked for a short time but he needed a constant supply to keep his truck running. We had a good laugh.

At this time there was a Polish man called Raminski. He was notorious for escaping having absconded from jail about four times. During one of his escapes the police were stopping all the traffic just north of Inverness. Wattie Dey was in front and the police asked him if he had seem Raminski. Wattie thought he said Kamanski and told the police he was in that lorry at the back. Of course they made a mad dive for the truck. Eddie wondered what he had done wrong but they soon got it sorted out.

We sometimes had to drive lime from the Ullapool limeworks. That was an horrendous drive. The road from Strathpeffer was narrow with blind corners and passing places. If you went off the road you landed in peat. We didn't go off the road but we often passed a truck on its side or sunk into the peat. They were usually transporting lime. Most of the Ullapool lime went to farms in the Inverness and Black Isle area. Sometimes, if we were very late in finishing we would just kip down in a barn or shed, or just sleep in the lorry. One time, coming from Ullapool, we had a blow out in one of our tyres. We had no spare so we were stuck. We were quite near Muir of Ord where there was a large commercial garage called Ben Motors. I went in and spoke to a salesman to see if he had any second hand tyres as I had no money to buy new. He said 'No.' but we could open an account and buy a new tyre and be billed for it later. We did this and, because he had helped us and they were Dodge agents, we bought quite a few Dodge lorries from him afterwards, so his good deed paid off.

The lorries we had were both petrol so we decided we would buy one with a diesel engine which would be much more economical as diesel was cheaper and we would get more miles to the gallon. We heard that Riddochs Timber Merchants, Rothiemay, had a four wheel Albion HD53 for sale which we went and looked at and bought. It was unusual as it was fitted with a six cylinder Albion engine which was normally only fitted to multi wheel vehicles. I think that it would maybe have been built for pulling a trailer.

Another problem was that, as we didn't have a tipper truck all our loads had to be emptied with shovels into the lime spreader. We decided to invest in a tipper so went into Aberdeen and round the dealers. We found one about our price range, a Thornycroft Sturdy Diesel, fitted with a Saurer diesel engine. I think they were made in Sweden. Unfortunately it turned out to be a complete disaster, just no end of trouble. At the same time we bought a Nuffield tractor fitted with a loader so now we could tip the lime and then load it on to the spreader. By this time we had bought another lime spreader. It was fitted on to an ex Army Chevrolet four by four, exactly the same as I had driven when I was employed at Parkmore. All we needed now was another truck fitted with a tipper. In the meantime I drove the big Albion which didn't have a tipper so the lime had to be emptied by hand until one day, I was coming out of Burghead with a load and landed in the ditch. The cab just fell to bits round about me. We did manage to drive it home without a cab. We did eventually build a new cab but it was pretty rough. We used old bed angles for the framework all welded together with a welder which we had built out of a 30 volt high amperage ex-aeroplane generator driven by an engine. We didn't even have a welding mask. We used old fashioned glass photo negatives, so little wonder it was so rough. In fact we never did use that lorry again. We replaced it with an ex-Forestry Commission Bedford Tipper with a petrol engine, but most of the time we used paraffin. We started it on petrol then when it was hot we went on to paraffin which was much cheaper than petrol.

The Capital Lime Co. was owned by a man by the name of Joe Flaherty. He lived in Edinburgh and employed his brother Bob, who lived in Aberdeen as area manager for the north. The company was called Capital because the head office was in Edinburgh. In fact they didn't own anything. They employed salesmen all over Scotland going round the farms selling lime to the farmers. They also sold slag which came into Aberdeen in bags by boat. It was terrible, dirty stuff to work with. They then started shipping coal into Burghead Harbour for the gas works in Elgin and we delivered this as well. The contract with the gas works was with Hargreaves, an English firm owning coal mines, among other things. In order to keep our contract licence within the law the coal was sold to the Capital Lime Co. on paper and bought back by Hargreaves as soon as we went through the Gas Works gate, just bending the law ever so slightly. We were now looking to replace that useless heap of scrap, the Thorneycroft, and I had heard of a diesel Commer in Nicholson's Garage in Elgin. We went to see it and asked Mr. Nicholson if he would be interested in a part exchange with the Thorneyfield. He told us to bring it in and he would see if he would do a deal. As we needed to tidy the lorry up a bit I said we would bring it in next week as it was away down south. When he heard that he said, 'Oh, so it's not just a heap of junk.'

We went home to give it a tidy up. One of the problems was that the cab around the radiator was all rusted away. Lying around was a roll of strong paper, ex-MOD stuff that I had picked up at a government sale. It was like two sheets of paper with tarry stuff in between. We set about and patched all the rusted bits with the paper and then painted over it. We then threw lime dust over it so that it didn't look like a recent job. At the garage we did the deal, we couldn't afford to have any scruples then but Nicholson had a bit of a reputation so I have no doubt the Thorneycroft probably didn't cost him much.

Occasionally we would have to deliver an order for hot lime, that is, lime that has been burned in a kiln. We had to collect it from a place called Green Loaming in England. It was terrible stuff to work with. If it got on your skin and you had been sweating it would burn. It was particularly bad round the nose, mouth and eyes, anywhere damp. We didn't have masks but I did sometimes tie a handkerchief over my mouth which did help, but many a night I went home with no skin on my nose and mouth. I'm sure it didn't do our lungs any good either. Loading the lorries at the lime works was also a right Heath Robinson affair. Two men loaded the burned lime, sometimes still hot out of the kiln, into barrows which we then had to navigate up a narrow plank into a crusher. Our lorry would be standing underneath the crusher. It took about four hours to load the two lorries.

When we went south with the petrol Bedford we used a drop of petrol poured into the manifold to start the engine, then on to paraffin. We used to carry extra fuel in cans and once, when on the way home, we stopped and filled the lorry tank just before going into Edinburgh as there was no by-pass at that time. Some of the tins must have had muck in them as right in the middle of Princess Street the Bedford came to a sudden stop, I knew it was a fuel problem. There I was, stuck in four lanes of traffic, second lane from the left. I had no option but to dismantle the carburettor and clean it out. My fear was that if the engine cooled down too much it wouldn't start on paraffin. I was really panicking. My two brothers were behind me in the diesel Commer with a line of traffic behind them, so close that they couldn't move out to the next lane. I just had to ignore the horns blowing. I'm not sure how long I took to clear the blockage but I think it must have been less than ten minutes. I pressed the starter and away she went with a cloud of smoke which filled the street. We were very lucky as we didn't see a policeman.

It was a two day job then, to go to England. I remember going down three times in one week and changing a spring in between. When we did get tired we just crawled under the cover and had a short sleep lying on the lime. One time we were sent to Aberdeen to collect slag off a boat and deliver it to farms in Aberdeenshire. My brother Gordon was only seventeen at the time and you had to be eighteen before you could drive a lorry if its unladen weight was more than three tons. He was driving one of the Maudsleys which weighed in about five tons unladen. Going through Forfar a car passed him and then turned sharply across in front of him. Gordon didn't stand a chance and ran completely over the top of the car. The driver managed to crawl out of the back window unhurt. The police arrived at the scene and when my brother was asked his name he gave them his older brother's name, David Baillie. He was given a ticket to produce his driving license and insurance at Elgin Police Station. David duly went and showed his papers the next day. The car driver was charged and pleaded guilty, which was just as well as David would have had to appear in court, so we got away with that.

Another episode I remember well, we were spreading lime at a farm just off the Elgin to Rothes road called Barrluick with a very steep road. My brother Gordon was driving the Commer truck with David coming behind with the Nuffield tractor with a front loader bucket. The tractor jumped out of gear and took off down the steep brae and no brakes to stop with. All David could do was aim the bucket so that it would connect with the chassis of Gordon's truck. When he collided with the truck Gordon got a real fright and the jolt nearly broke his neck. Luckily there was no serious damage done but the bucket had cut into the chassis by about six inches.

About 1960 I heard that my old boss, Robert Paterson, was hiring lorries as he had opened a quarry near Elgin. I went to see him and he said I could start right away. He gave me a written contract there and then and although, by law, we should have waited for a licence to be granted, we started the next day.

We decided to buy a new lorry for this job so I contacted SMT, the Bedford agents, in Aberdeen. We had decided to part exchange the big Albion with the home built cab and they sent a salesman to see it. We did a deal and took delivery of a new lorry more or less right away. Ian Anderson, who had been employed by me in the firewood business, became the driver and he was left to get on with it. He just had to report to the office at the concrete block factory at Kingston and he would be directed from there. We, meanwhile, carried on with the lime. The lime company was beginning to worry us though as the payments were becoming irregular. As they got later and later we became pretty strapped for money. There was no option but to carry on but we were looking out for other openings. I had my eye on Robert Paterson's lorries because the manager at the block works, Fred Cruickshank, said he was fed up with them always breaking down. They had five lorries but usually only three of them were on the road at any one time. They had all seen better days. I happened to be at the office in Newmill of Keith collecting an account for the work we were doing and asked Mr. Paterson if it would not be a better idea to contract out all his haulage. He said that was not a bad idea but that he would have to think about it. Well, a couple of days later he asked me to go to his office and said that he was interested but to get the contract I would have to take over his lorries, pretty much what I had expected. I was told to go home and do my sums and go back with a price per ton for delivery of his goods based on a radius from his block factory and his quarry, the rate changing every five miles. To be honest, I didn't have a clue where to start. I went to see my friend Fred Cruickshank, the manager at the block factory, and he gave me a copy of the existing rates. This was, for me, just like finding a pot of gold. I got stuck in and worked out a price based on the copy but increasing most of the prices so that he wouldn't know I had seen them. He had special prices for areas where he had competitors but I ignored that. I went to his office and presented my rates. He studied them for a few minutes then said, 'You are right on the firing line.' In fact he didn't change any of my prices except to ask for a special rate for anywhere with competitors so we managed to come to an agreement. The next thing was to agree on a price for his lorries. He suggested we get two independent people to value them. I got a salesman from SMT in Aberdeen and Mr. Paterson got Forbes the

Albion agents, also from Aberdeen. There was quite a big difference in the valuations so we just agreed to a price halfway between and the deal was done. He also agreed that we could pay the lorries so much off our account every month which was a great help. The trucks involved were three four wheel Maudsleys, one four wheel Albion and one eight wheel AEC. We applied for the 'A Contract' licences needed before we could start. That only took about three weeks and then we were in business.

We had always done all our own repairs, but with five extra trucks which were not in the best of condition, we often had to work all night to get a truck going for morning. To add to our problems as we didn't have a garage all our repairs had to be done in the open.

My younger brother, Gordon, doing some repairs to an engine out in the open. Note the oil drum for a bench. In the picture, top right, is an eight wheel AEC.

One of the Maudsley trucks with driver, Fred Fraser.

We eventually got the use of a derelict house right in the centre of Kingston belonging to Mr. Paterson. He let us knock the end out but, of course, we could only get one truck in at any one time. We managed to stay there for about six months before the planning people cottoned on that we hadn't applied for planning permission. I expect there would have been a few complaints from our neighbours so I don't think we would have got it anyway. In the meantime we were trying to get other premises. In Garmouth a man by the name of Arthur Scott had a bus on a school contract. He was much like ourselves, struggling all the time to pay his accounts. There was no MOT test for trucks back then but public service vehicles had to be tested. Whenever his bus was due for testing he used to come to us and borrow wheels and tyres, just to get his bus passed, and then return them. He also had a piece of ground in Garmouth and had obtained outline planning permission for a garage and petrol filling station. He had borrowed the money from the Shell Petrol Co. and they delivered to the site two one thousand gallon fuel tanks and two petrol pumps. The holes were dug ready for the tanks but then, sadly, he went out of business. As we also dealt with Shell for our fuel the area manager gave us the chance to buy the ground and equipment as they had the titles for the ground. All they wanted was the amount of money owed to them being fifty pounds. Of course we jumped at the chance and bought the ground, the tanks and the pumps as well. All we needed now was a building for the site. Robert Paterson, as well as having a cement block factory and builders business, also bought and sold ex-military huts. He had just bought a camp at Alness so we went to see the huts and bought one. It just consisted of steel trusses and corrugated iron sheeting. We dismantled it ourselves and transported it home. Walter Leith Building Contractor, Grange, did the mason work, the rest we did ourselves.

Our garage at Garmouth. The rounded roof is the original. The extra building on the left was added later. The house, far left, was my mother's, built when our father died in 1961. The croft at Grange was sold.

One of our earlier trucks. It was in a head on collision with another truck belonging to an Aberdeen firm. The driver, John Gordon was not hurt but the truck was a write-off.

By this time the lime contract had come to an end. We had a substantial account outstanding with the company. I phoned them a few times but no joy. So I hired a car, as the one I had was not very reliable, and went down to their office in Princes St. Edinburgh, more or less across from the castle, to see if I could get some of our money. I actually didn't have much hope but I thought I had to try. Happily, they gave me a cheque for the full amount. I couldn't get home fast enough to see if the cheque would go through and it did. It was a very good move on my part because just a week after that they stopped trading. We were very lucky because a lot of the other contractors lost out.

By this time we had about nine lorries working with Paterson and as he was expanding all the time we had to grow with him. The bank we were with was in Garmouth and the banker was very good to us but when the Garmouth branch closed we were transferred to the Fochabers branch which was a different kettle of fish altogether. We had no end of hassle. At that time our overdraft limit was only four thousand pounds but in reality I could never get below about six thousand pounds. Eventually the banker asked for a meeting. He came down to Garmouth and wanted to know when I could reduce the overdraft to the limit. I said it was just about impossible so he asked me to sell one of our lorries. I couldn't believe what I was hearing as that would have been a backward step. The meeting was on a Friday and he said that he would be back the following Friday to see what I had done about it. I was really worried so I went to see my accountant Mr. Harry Clark. He said, 'You don't have to take all that hassle because you are their customer and there are other banks.' He set up an urgent meeting with the manager of the Clydesdale Bank on the Monday afternoon. I went to the meeting armed with the balance sheets for the last two years which showed quite good results. The banker studied them for a few minutes, asked a few questions and said right away that on the basis of those balance sheets he would be prepared to give me an overdraft of ten thousand pounds and if circumstances changed in the future to come back and we could work something out. We had some standing orders for lorries on hire purchase which he said, if we would bring the paperwork to him, he would sort out. He also gave me a cheque to pay off the debt to the other bank and close the account the following Monday. The Fochabers banker duly appeared on the Friday and said, 'What have you done about this overdraft?' I said, 'Quite a lot. I will be issuing you with a cheque for the full amount owed on Monday.' He replied, 'That's capital. How did you manage that?' I replied, 'You don't need to know that because I will be closing my account as from Monday.' Well, he just about had a fit and tried to make me change my mind. He said if I had asked for an increase in my overdraft they could have matched any other bank. If that was the case why hadn't he advised me of that? I said that it was now too late. After all the hassle and worry I had I really enjoyed telling him what to do with his overdraft. To this day the firm are still with the Clydesdale Bank. By the way, the Fochabers banker's name was Mr. Stoney and he was widely known as Mr. Stoney Broke.

At this time I was running an Austin A55 car. One day, with a gale blowing, I had to open the boot. The wind caught it and tore it off breaking the hinges. I didn't bother to repair it. As well as that the brakes were defective. If you wanted to stop you had to pump the pedal. In Elgin going up the brae over the railway bridge towards New

Elgin, a landrover in front of me had to stop quickly. I didn't have time to pump the pedal so I ran into the back of it. The driver jumped out and said that he was so sorry, he hadn't realised that he had let his vehicle run back. I didn't make him any the wiser. He gave me the name of his insurance company but I didn't have the hard neck to claim. Shortly after, I was following one of our Dodge trucks up our own road and the driver stopped just in front of my house. Again I didn't have time to pump the pedal so I ran into the back of the truck and that was the end of that car.

By 1962 we had fourteen tippers, seven Dodge trucks and seven Ford Thames trucks, all bought new but the Fords were giving us a lot of trouble. The Dodge was a first class truck as long as they were fitted with the Perkins 6/354 engine. Six years on and we still had seven Dodges on the road but no Fords as they only lasted about three years at the most. Then Bert Paterson sold his business to Builders' Merchants, MacGruther and Marshall. This was far better for us as Bertie was always short of money and often when I went for payment he would post date the cheque to the following week, presumably to give him time to get the money in. MacGruther and Marshall then decided to move into ready mix concrete and approached us to see if we would be interested in buying concrete mixers for them to hire. Of course we said yes. I went down to a Readymix place near Bristol and bought three eight wheel Fodens. We wished afterwards that we hadn't gone near them. They were fitted with Foden's own two stroke diesel engine and they were a disaster. They had six cylinders and each one had a single cylinder head which used to crack between the valves. In fact we used to train the drivers how to change the head, which took less than half an hour, and they carried spare heads in the cab. We got the cracked ones welded. That wasn't the only problem. On top of the pistons was what was called the firing ring. They used to break and that cylinder then stopped firing. Of course we were running grossly overloaded. The unladen weight was about fifteen tons and we were carrying a pay load of twenty tons – a gross weight of thirty five tons. The legal weight was twenty four tons. The police and the traffic examiners often pulled our other trucks in and weighed them but never bothered with the mixers. I suppose they thought it wasn't possible to overload them.

We also bought an AEC mixer giving us a total of five. I must tell this story which could have had horrendous consequences. We were just very lucky. My brother Gordon, at that time in charge of the garage, decided to make an apparatus to wash the trucks. It consisted of a cylinder which held about one hundred gallons of water connected to the air line with the compressor set to twenty pounds per square inch. It worked very well until one day, unknown to me, James Branson was washing his mixer and a man came in to get his car tyres checked. I went into the garage, screwed up the compressor and was checking the tyres when there was an almighty crash just behind me inside the garage. The cylinder had split at the welding, the bottom being left on the ground. Somebody in the village who saw it go up said it disappeared into low clouds just like a rocket. Some other folk saw it coming down and thought it had come off an aeroplane. It crashed through the roof of the garage some five feet from me and landed on top of the compressor, which was only slightly damaged. James Branson was left with just the hose in his hand and dived under the truck for safety. That was the end of that apparatus, although it would have worked fine if we had fitted a reducer in the line (not a factory inspector in sight).

We had four Foden mixers with two stroke engines. I think we had four too many because they were no end of trouble. To explain, the working of the two stroke engine, unlike a four stroke which fires every second stroke, the two stroke fires every stroke. To get rid of the burned gasses there were two vent holes halfway up the cylinder. One is the exhaust and the other is connected to a blower which blows air into the cylinder blowing the gasses out of the exhaust. It also fills the cylinder with fresh air which mixes with the diesel and then fires. I had to explain the principle of the two stroke engine so that you could understand the following repair which my brother Gordon carried out. The mixer driver, James Branson, was delivering ready mix to a farm up at Mulben

One of the Fodens with James Branson, the driver.
This truck came to grief when the tipper ram broke with a full tipper.

The driver, Gordon MacLean, was lucky as he was in the cab at the time.

near Keith when he phoned home to say that the Foden had developed a serious knock in the engine. I sent my brother Gordon to see what was wrong. When he reached the scene and heard the knock he knew right away it was serious. He dropped the sump and discovered one of the big ends had gone. Something had to be done before the concrete set. He removed the cylinder head, then the piston and con rod. He was hoping that he could get to the destination, which was only about a quarter of a mile away, and get rid of the load. He pressed the starter but no joy. It suddenly dawned on him what was wrong, all the air from the blower was escaping out of that cylinder. They tried to stuff rags into the hole but all that happened was that the rags were blown out and got tangled up on the crank shaft. He walked up to the farm to see if he could find anything to block the hole. The first thing he saw just lying there was a ball which the children had been playing with. Looking at it he thought it was just about the right size so he grabbed it, went back to the mixer and pushed the ball into the cylinder. It was a tight fit but just what was needed. He pressed the starter and the engine burst into life. The load was delivered, just in time as the cement was just beginning to set, and the truck towed home.

My wife and I had now been living in the old bus for ten years. Our eldest girl, Jane, was now ten years old so it was getting pretty crowded. I heard there was a firm dismantling prefabricated houses in Anderson Drive, Aberdeen. They had been imported from America and built during the war. The outer walls were flat sheet asbestos. An apex roof, but nearly flat and covered with very thick felt. I went and had a look and was quite impressed with them. Fifty pounds was the price, all dismantled and ready to uplift, so I bought one. My father also bought one to use for a henhouse. He only used half so I bought the other half from him which gave me an extra bedroom because with two boys and two girls we needed three bedrooms. We then had to get planning permission, which back then was no problem and got on with laying the foundations. The house was all in sections and my wife and I built it more or less by ourselves, although we had to get a hand with the roof sections as they were pretty heavy. After we built the house we got an account from the Water Board for six pounds for water they said we must have used. We had used water from a private well when we stayed in the bus and I said I was not going to pay. Then an official appeared and he said all water in Morayshire belonged to Laich of Moray Water Board even if it came out of a ditch. In fact, as a matter of principal, I never did pay that six pounds.

As soon as we had a bit more money, we built concrete blocks around the prefab, leaving the asbestos still in place. We also acquired trusses and re-roofed it over the top of the felt and tar. After that you would never know that it had once been a prefab in Aberdeen. At first we didn't have mains electricity because we couldn't afford it. The Hydro Board transformer was quite a bit away and would have needed four poles and cost about four hundred pounds. I picked up a twenty four volt generator which charged the two twelve volt batteries we kept in the house. I also bought an aeroplane rotary converter giving 240 volts, just enough to power a small TV and two forty watt bulbs. It didn't last long though as the batteries produced gas while charging and you had to be very careful and not cause a spark. I forgot, and removed the cable which caused a spark and both batteries blew to bits. The acid went up in the air and, by good luck, it missed my face. It came down and landed on my back. I immediately pulled off my shirt before the acid reached my skin. The shirt had hundreds of holes in it and had to be binned. That was the end of that apparatus.

I then acquired a six horse power Lister engine and knew where to get a 240 generator. I mated the generator to the engine and I had electricity. The engine had to be hand cranked to start and it was pretty hard work. I had to put some oil into the intake to give it some compression for starting. I also had to take the spring off the governors and then replace it after it was started. This worked quite well until one time I forgot to replace the spring and went into the house. Everything was OK because we had a double element heater going which kept the engine from running off. Then the room got hot and my wife switched off the heater. When the load on the engine was removed, it took off. The first that we knew that all was not well was when the light bulbs started blowing to bits and some of the cables were burning. The wife was screaming so I ran out to the shed where the engine was. It was running flat out so I grabbed the cable connected to the batteries and at the same time grabbed the stop on the engine with my other hand. As I did so 240 volts shot through me and there I was, stuck. I've had lots of shocks in my time but never anything like that. How I wasn't killed I'll never know. I then contacted the Hydro Board to see about getting the power to our house. That took them about three months so we worked away with the engine until then. I tell you, I never forgot to attach the spring again.

(left) is the prefab house as it was when we built it. The door far left was the coal house.

(below) is the same house as it is today with the new roof which I built on over the top of the old and my daughter, Ann, who bought the house in 1976 made the coal house into a dining room. She also made another room in the attic so now it's a four bedroom house with double glazing and central heating.Underneath it all, the original prefab is still intact.

This is the next house I built where I still live.

Doris feeding the pheasants she had tamed in front of the house.

Ann had been dating Doug Morrison for quite a while and they were engaged to be married and had set the date. When the big day came, because she was our transport manager, we thought it would be fitting if she was taken from the Church in Garmouth after the ceremony to the St. Andrews Hotel in Lhanbryde for the reception in one of the lorries. It would be a good advertisement for Baillie Brothers (I never miss a trick). We used a truck which was just weeks old with Billy Seivewright driving.

When Ann and Doug married they needed a house and as I had been toying with the idea of building another house for a while and had the

(left) Doug and Ann's blackening

(right) Doug and Ann's wedding.

and, I decided to go ahead. I decided on a site where a house had been standing before although all that was left was a heap of stones. I set about getting planning permission which was not a problem because of the house having been there already. As I was so well connected to the building trade I was able to pick up a lot of materials for very little. For example, we did a lot of work for Crudens house builders who at that time had quite a few house building projects, mainly at Lossiemouth and Nairn, and we had done all the excavations and supplied them with all their transport needs. When the contract at Lossiemouth ended we got the contract to clean up the site including removal of a shed which had been a store for building materials. Inside was about 100 sheets of plasterboard, some slightly damaged by water, so instead of going to the dump they were taken home to my own housing project. Scattered about was quite a few concrete blocks and lengths of timber, all of use for my house. After I gathered most of the materials needed I got some masons to build the blocks, all as homers at weekends, and just paid them with cash on the Sunday night. I did the same with the joiners and, in total, the whole house, complete with new furniture, cost just under £14,000.

After we finished building the house, we went into Elgin to the Furniture Discount Centre to buy the furniture. Doris just picked me up at the garage and I had my working clothes on which were a bit greasy, I probably looked like a down and out. We went into the shop and Doris said, 'I'll have that, and that, and that...' The account was mounting up and the shop owner, Derek Galt, with whom I eventually became very good friends, told me afterwards that, as the bill was mounting up, he was thinking, 'How is this tramp going to manage to pay for all this?' He said he learned that day to never go by appearances. Derek was like ourselves as his premises in Station Road, Elgin, was too small for the amount of trade he was doing so he bought premises in South Street, Elgin, which consisted of a grocer's shop and two derelict houses. He set about building the whole lot into a two storey shop, doing most of the work himself. Derek had always some project on hand. One of them was building a fishing boat as he had come from a fishing family. He was looking for a place to build it and I said that he could build it beside my house as I had plenty of room and he would have access to any tools and electricity. He bought a steel shell and proceeded to build it from there. I think it took him about two years. My family and I quite enjoyed watching it develop from a steel shell into a 30ft fishing boat.

This is the boat just after painting. It was sand blasted first. The blaster is sitting in the foreground. In the background is my shed which he used occasionally. Further back is the roof of my house.

A crane lifting the boat on to a low loader to transport it to Burghead Harbour

Doris had acquired four hens and a cockerel from a friend who was moving house and had no room to keep hens. Eventually one of the hens disappeared and only turned up occasionally at feeding time. We didn't buy any feed, they only got scraps from the kitchen but they were allowed to roam about anywhere so got plenty of seeds. I knew that this particular hen was laying away but couldn't find her. She eventually appeared with twelve chickens which turned out to be eight hens and four cockerels so we had twelve laying hens. We sold the surplus eggs to a local butcher. One time we were going on a picnic and Doris hard boiled six eggs. Someone came to visit us so we didn't get to go on the picnic. When the butcher came Doris had two dozen eggs for him and, by mistake, the six hard boiled eggs were amongst them. We fully expected to hear about this but never did. Someone got six ready cooked eggs. Doris never told the butcher.

Along the Moray coast where we lived the weather was very good. We hardly ever had any snow although we did get pretty bad frost. What we do get which is worse than any snow is sand blowing. The photographs show the damage the sand did to our garden. Doris was so cut up about her garden as it was looking really well. She lived for her garden and really loved her flowers and this was really heartbreaking for her. After this episode I built a higher wall which, although it didn't stop it completely it made a big difference. At the weekend all the family mucked in and cleared most of the sand away. Most of the plants, though, were destroyed except, the heather which survived.

I picked up an old Austin 7 car, it wasn't really roadworthy but I thought the bairns would get a bit of fun from it. Jane would have been about eleven, John ten, Ann nine and William eight so I bolted blocks of wood on to the pedals so they could reach them. There was plenty of room for them to run about with it as we were the only house in the area and about half a mile from the nearest public road. They had a great time with it. My wife's father and mother came down to stay with us for a few days and the children were shouting to get their grandfather, Bill Ross, to go with them for a hurl. Eventually, he went and, of course, they had to show off a wee bit. John was driving and he ran down a small tree which sprang, back lifting the wheels off the ground on one side. They were stuck so I had to go and help them get it down. Bill was absolutely terrified and said he would never go into that car again. Eventually it gave up the ghost and they started to take it to bits and sold some of the parts. I do remember that they sold the head lamps but I can't remember what else they sold. Good learning for them.

We did a lot of work for Morrison Construction and my brother Gordon was very good friends with Ian Mackie, who was in charge of Morrison Plant division and there was a lot of good humoured banter between them.

One day a letter arrived in our office addressed to Gordon. (below)

This is John and William who had great fun with the Austin seen in the background.

MORRISON PLANT

Registered Office: Shandwick House, Chapel Street, Tain, Ross-shire IV19 1JF
Telephone (0862) 2202   Telex 75408

Part of the Morrison Construction Group

Our Ref: IRM/WM

10th August 1987

Baillie Brothers
Station Road
Garmouth
Morayshire

Dear Sir

Tae the Heid Bummer

Fir a whiley noo, Ive bin a bittie ungshis aboot your kepacity
tae rin yer placey.

Hiven hooiniver hid a squintie o'a broshoor thit cum fae IVIKO,
istreen, Ive jaloosed yer problem.

Ye dinna hae sifichint folkies wrochtin fur ye.

Noo yiv bin telt. Tak heid, Knipe on.

Gan ye tae I broo doon bye an get a puckle dizin buggers yokit.

Tak sum foties an mak up a funcie pumflit.

Ging abbot like SH.T. af a shuvel gein awa moturs tae a hoor in
sicht. (In sum hoo-ur oot o sicht).

Noo if on the ither han ye ging bang fur want o siller.

Weel weel

Ye niver wer muckle ees ony wye.

THE MANNIE

82

Gordon asked if I would write a reply which I did. (right)

The business was now doing well and we kept expanding. The Mayne quarry at Elgin was mostly sand but Bertie opened a quarry at Coleburn which was situated about six miles from Elgin on the Elgin to Rothes road. We had to drive the gravel from there to the crusher at Mayne. That needed three trucks which could also take a back load when returning making it a good earner. We also had to keep the concrete block factory at Kingston supplied which kept one truck busy full time. All the trucks returning home at the end of the day took back loads keeping them supplied.

BAILLIE BROS. (Cont.) Ltd.

SPECIALISTS TIPPER TRUCKS BULK POWDER TANKERS	**Haulage Contractors** GARMOUTH : MORAYSHIRE Telephone: SPEY BAY 312 / 313 *Directors: J. Baillie, G. Baillie, D. Baillie*	DEMOLITION EXCAVATION ROCK HAULAGE

TAE THE MANNIE AT MORRISONS

FIN THIS SCRIBBLE 'O' YOURS CAAM HERE TAE OOR PLACIE,
THE QUINES IN THE OFFICE WAR NEAR PACKEN THEIR CASIE;
THEY THOCHT AD GOTTEN WARK FOR MA LARRIES IN TIAWAN,
AN THEY WERE THINKEN IT WISNA A GWEED PLAN.

FOR THE QUINES IN OOR OFFICE ARE A HAGGIS TRAPPERS,
AN AM SOME FEART YER LETTER IS A IN TATTERS,
THEY TRIED TAE READ IT BACK THE WYE,
AN THEY TRIED TAE READ IT DOON THE WYE.

ANE 'O' THEM COOKED UP A PLAN OR SO SHE THOCHT,
A WEE SHOT 'O' ALEX'S GLESSES SHE SOCHT,
BIT THAT DIDNA HELP HER READIN AVA,
AN SHE SAYS "A TAE HELL A THINK ALL AWA".

THIS IVIKO BROOSHER THAT YE BUNGED DOON TAE ME,
IF A SAID A WIS IMPRESSED A WID BE TELLIN A LEE,
NAE WINNER THEIR LARRIES COST THOOSANS 'O' POWNS,
FIN THEY HIV TAE PEY SILLER TAE SIC A BOORACH 'O' CLOWNS.

WE NOO HIV OOR BROOSHER IN A FUNCIE BINDER,
BIT A DOOT A DOOT WEIL HAE TAE GANG WIDER,
FOR THE HOORS ROON HERE ARE FEW AN FAR ATWEEN,
COS THEY NOO A BIDE IN THE TOON 'O' ABERDEEN.

FOR WINT 'O' BAWBEES WEIL NAE GING PLUNK,
COS THERE'S AYE PLENTY SILLER TAE BE GOT FAE THE BAUNK,
ALL HAE TAE GING AN WARK NOO, THAT ILL HAE TAE DEE,
JIST IN CASE THE BAUNKER DECIDES TAE BUNG AWA THE KEY.

Elgin Building Services opened another quarry at the Cloddach on the Elgin to Dallas road about three miles from Elgin and closed the Mayne Quarry and the Coleburn Quarry.

Photograph of lorries taken about 1964.

Big dumper being repaired by John.

We were then asked to provide off the road dumpers to work on site feeding the crusher. I went down south again and bought two Foden dumpers with a carrying capacity of thirty five tons each. Elgin Building Services also had another rock quarry at Netherglen where they made tar macadam and wanted a dumper to feed the crusher there as well. I bought a smaller one for that job. Eventually the concrete block factory was moved from Kingston to the Cloddach. Feeding the factory at Kingston had been a good earner for us but, of course, it made good sense for them to have everything in one place.

MacGruther and Marshall also supplied bulk cement which was collected from Inverness railway station where Blue Circle had silos. Four bulk tankers were engaged on this and MacGruther and Marshall asked if we would take over their four tankers, two ERF and two Dodge's which we did. It turned out to be a very good earner and we still have that contract today.

Tanker in trouble.

We were transporting special cement that would harden under water from England when the driver caught the soft at Calvine on the A9, easily done. It was a drivers nightmare. Twenty tons of very expensive cement lost but the main thing was the driver was ok.

Another firm took over from MacGruther and Marshall called Elgin Building Services. They eventually supplied their own cement mixers. We were quite pleased about this as that part of our business had just been a nightmare from start to finish, mostly due to the Foden two stroke engine. The Foden,

One of the latest tankers.

unlike other mixers which had a donkey engine to drive the drum, had a hydraulic engine with the pump driven off the power take off.

Our next move was to buy over a plant hire business from a man in Deskford, Alistair Bowie. The plant consisted of three Case tracked excavators, a TD6 International and a wheeled loading shovel. Instead of applying for excavator drivers we decided to train some of our existing drivers. We picked three of the ex-ready mix drivers who were now driving tippers. Alistair Macintosh, Fred Fraser, James Branson and other drivers as they became available were sent down to the beach at Kingston and told to play among the gravel until they became familiar with the machines. We never regretted doing this as all of them became first class machine drivers. Fred was on the International, which we didn't keep very long as it had seen better days and was replaced with a new Bristol Taurus crawler.

Fred and the Bristol.

Fred was a first class driver and could turn his hand to just about anything. We also taught the machine drivers electric welding in the same way we taught them to drive the machines. We gave them a box of welding rods and some scrap bits of metal and told them to spend a day practicing welding. This was very useful as when the bucket teeth or the tracks needed building up the drivers could manage the job themselves. Very cost effective.

The Case in trouble.

In 1970 the licensing laws changed. The 'A' and 'A Contract', 'B' and 'C' licensing was replaced with the 'O' licence which allowed us to haul any kind of goods anywhere for anybody. This was a great improvement over the old system where we were tied to one customer only.

A 'C' licence which only allowed us to haul our own goods.

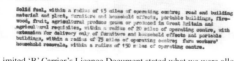
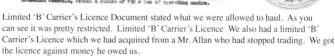

Limited 'B' Carrier's Licence Document stated what we were allowed to haul. As you can see it was pretty restricted. Limited 'B' Carrier's Licence We also had a limited 'B' Carrier's Licence which we had acquired from a Mr. Allan who had stopped trading. We got the licence against money he owed us.

The 'A Contract' which only allowed us to haul goods for the firm we had a contract with. We were not even allowed to haul our own goods.

Ann Baillie, transport manager, now Mrs. Morrison.

Brenda Baillie, my youngest daughter, now Mrs. MacBain, who took over from Ann.

As the restricted licences were now all replaced by an 'O' licence we were now in a good position to compete with other hauliers. We could take on earth moving jobs and we had the means to excavate and load the trucks. We specialized in tippers, always connected to building trade and public works. We never tried to compete with long distance traffic. Once when we were short of work we tried hauling grain to the maltings but we could not make it pay. The biggest problem was the queue of trucks waiting to be emptied, sometimes waiting up to three hours. Better to park the trucks and pay drivers off. We seldom had to do that.

In 1973 we started to haul sand and gravel for a large contract at Lossiemouth Aerodrome. They were using over a thousand tons a day. We had to hire up to forty trucks as well as our own so this job was a good earner on its own as we charged ten per cent. My second daughter Ann was transport manager then and on one day we had, including

our own thirty trucks, eighty four trucks operating. Ann had trucks hired from all over Aberdeen, Inverness and even Motherwell and Bridge of Earn. We managed to renew nearly all of our fleet from that job. By this time we had become the local agent for Foden trucks.

Snow ploughs supplied to Highland Region.

The lorry seven from the right with an apparatus sticking up is in fact a high-ab lift which was used for loading and unloading concrete blocks most of the time. The driver was Billy Seivewright. One of the few times Billy was not on the blocks he was driving infill into a development at the

This is our fleet of thirty two trucks, mostly all Fodens, taken in 1974 after we had renewed most of them.

Wards in Elgin. He had just put up his tipper when there was a loud bang. A few seconds later another, and then another. Six in all, he was completely mystified and frightened. It turned out that he was under a high voltage cable, four thousand volts, and although the truck was about six feet under the cable the high voltage jumped on to the top of his tipper box, down through the chassis, earthing through the steel in the tyres where the heat burst them one at a time. We claimed off the insurance company but I had a difficult time convincing the rep what had happened. When they eventually checked they found there had been a previous claim in the past for the same thing so our claim was successful. That wasn't the end of the story though because as time went on we had to replace most of the wheel bearings as they had been damaged by the high voltage passing through them. The driver was lucky as the Fodens had fibreglass cabs. If it had been a steel cab the electricity would have earthed through his body when he jumped out and he would not have survived four thousand volts.

In 1970 a man by the name of Jack Noble opened a haulage business in Elgin. His father, apparently, was a coal merchant and haulage contractor in Aberdeen but he created havoc in Elgin by cutting prices. He knocked a few haulage men out of business, especially in work connected with distilleries and long distance. We weren't involved to begin with as most of our work was with the building trade and public works but he eventually began to affect us. Noble wined and dined MacGruther and Marshall's area manager and was even hired by them one Saturday afternoon when I had trouble getting men. I'm sure Noble thought that he had finally made an inroad to our business, maybe money passed hands, but the two of them didn't realize how friendly I was with the overall manager a Mr. Harry Wallace. When he heard about it he put a stop to it right away. He was a real toff. He came from a family of mine owners and still had an interest in open cast mines in the Birmingham area. He had a house in Fort William but spent a lot of his time in Elgin and, to a lesser extent, on his business interests in Birmingham. Jack Noble never did manage to bother us and in fact went out of business in the eighties. He has been deceased for a long time.

By now we had grown out of our garage and needed to build a bigger one. We wanted something second hand and made some enquiries. John Duncan, from Buckie, a good customer of ours supplied new and second hand buildings and said to leave it with him. He got back in touch to say he had found something suitable in England, steel work only. We asked him to go ahead and buy it and duly sent a truck down to collect it. To avoid disrupting repairs to our fleet we more or less just built over the top of the old garage. The job of erecting the steel work was contracted

(above) This was an ex-navy Coles crane fitted on to a Thorneycroft chassis bought for lifting the steelwork into place.

out to Alister Young Contractors, Fochabers and the masonry contract to Malcolm Philip. Malcolm was a real worthy, never sober. He used a lot of part-timers at weekends. How he avoided getting caught for drink driving I will never know. Spud Thompson was one of his part-timers who at that time worked for Wimpey. He told us a story about Malcolm Philip. One weekend he and Spud were going

The finished building.

to Rothes to do some work on the local minister's roof. When they got there the minister asked Malcolm if he would like a cup of tea or a dram. Malcolm answered, 'We'll have a dram until the tea is ready.' Spud eventually started up on his own and built up quite a successful builder's business.

We then got into the demolition business. There was never a conscious decision to start demolition we just seemed to drift into it. One of the first jobs was Cairnie Junction, near Huntly, which connected the main Aberdeen to Inverness line with the coast line which was closed in the Beeching cuts in the 1960s.

Cairnie Junction.

From left, Fred Fraser, J. Baillie (Jun.), William Thomson, James Branson, Gordon Baillie, myself, John Baillie, Gordon Smith, Billy Seivewright and William Baillie.

I certainly won't forget a house we demolished on the Roseisle to Kinloss road. It was a small house and very near the road. I thought I would save time by setting fire to it and getting rid of all the timber. It didn't half burn. I had omitted to notice, however, that the slates were asbestos which, if heated to a certain temperature, explodes into small pieces and they fly all over the place. As the house was so near the road, cars were being showered with pieces of asbestos. I was in a real panic, expecting to see the police arriving. They didn't, presumably nobody reported the incident. It only lasted about twenty minutes then the roof collapsed inside the walls which stopped the asbestos flying on to the road. We were lucky to get away with that caper.

We got a boost with the demolition when the father and son running a firm of public work and plant hire contractors fell out. They had disagreements quite regularly but then they had a real bust up and the son left to start on his own. The only plant he had was an old Drott so he approached us to see if he could hire our machines if he was successful in bidding for work. He got quite a few jobs and hired our earth moving machines regularly. He told me afterwards that his mother had told him the price his father had put in for different jobs so he was able to undercut him. Of course hiring us was just a stop gap until he could get plant of his own. He came to me with a schedule for the demolition of a few farm buildings, I think they were Crown farms. I did not have a clue how to start as I had not had much experience. I had only priced a few very small jobs and I told him so. He then said that he would teach me how to price jobs such as this which really was a great boost for our firm. Eventually he got plant of his own and he did well. We also went on to do an increasing number of demolition jobs. One job for Inverness county council was a disused school in Telford St., Inverness. There was a factory alongside which also had to go. It had a brick chimney eighty feet tall by about eight feet in diameter. This was a tricky business as there were houses all round. Once again I had to look around for someone's brains to pick. I remembered a customer of ours, Alex Arbuthnot, a contractor from Alves. We had carted rubble from a chimney he had demolished so I asked his advice. It was very simple, you just knock out a few bricks at the very bottom at the side in the direction you want it to fall, then put a rope round about half way up and pull with one of your machines. It worked a treat, the chimney landed exactly where we wanted. We were so busy then that we decided to work on it on a Sunday. We got a severe reprimand from the council offices who told us on no circumstances to work on a Sunday. All our subsequent contracts in or near Inverness had a clause inserted, no Sunday work.

Another demolition job for Inverness council we successfully bid for was the demolition of an ex wartime MOD camp at Dalcross, quite a big job for us. I always looked after any demolition jobs personally and as this job started at the same time as the school summer holidays Doris and I decided to take the four children and stay on the site. We had a caravan and we fixed up one of the smaller huts nearby for the children. We all stayed until the job was finished, a really interesting holiday for the children and they fair enjoyed it.

To explain the set up, I was in overall charge and looked after the haulage and plant hire side. My younger brother, David, looked after the garage night shift which we had started early on so that the trucks could be repaired overnight and ready for work during the day. My youngest brother, Gordon, was in charge of the workshop during the day. Both of them could take charge of the haulage side which they did from time to time and while I stayed at Dalcross. This was one of the better jobs as we made quite a profit. One incident happened with two bunkers built with very thick reinforced concrete, I suppose it would be bomb-proof. I hired a rope digger with a crane jib and borrowed what we called a bomb, which was a lump of metal, pear shaped, weighing about fifteen hundredweights and fixed by a chain to the digger rope. The procedure was to lift it as high up as possible and drop it onto what we wanted to break. This time it didn't make much impression as the concrete was too thick and to crown it all the chain broke and the bomb fell through one of the holes into eight feet of water. I then decided that we would have to blast them. Alistair Macintosh got a blaster's licence. I couldn't believe how easy it was for him to get the licence as although I didn't know very much about blasting I knew more than he did as I had been involved in blasting with plaster shots at Parkmore Limes. Alistair didn't even know how to insert the detonator into the gelignite, I had to show him. Every evening I had to go to a telephone to let them know at home how many trucks I would need the following day. Alistair was supposed to wait until I got back but took it upon himself to blast the bunker while I was away. There was a small hut about two hundred yards away used as a small factory. When I came back some of the windows were smashed. He had put too much gelignite on top of the bunker and not used enough wet earth to cover some of the 'shots' properly. This was after five p.m. so nobody was working in the factory. I went to see the owner next morning but as, apart from the windows, no other damage had been done and the building was being vacated the following week to be demolished, no more was said about it. We were lucky to get away with that. Needless to say I didn't let Alistair Mackintosh blast anything again.

Another demolition job that we had a wee problem with was at what had been Mains Garage and filling station in Lossiemouth. They had two underground petrol tanks which had to be dug out. We went ahead and lifted then as they were good tanks and took them back to our yard for storing diesel. I knew this would be dangerous as a tiny spark could have caused an explosion but one of the cement tankers had a blower and we used this to blow out all the fumes before moving them. After we had demolished the rest of the premises a man appeared and introduced himself as the Health and Safety Officer for Moray Council and he was there to see that we complied with the regulations regarding the lifting of the petrol tanks. I said we had already lifted them. He asked how had we got rid of the petrol fumes. I told him we had used the blower on one of our cement tankers. He was not very impressed and said we should have informed him when we were going to lift the tanks. And where were they anyway? I said we had cut them up and put them off for scrap. He nearly had a fit and gave me such a telling off about the dangers of empty tanks and petrol fumes.

We very often got GV9s after getting stopped at Ministry road checks. One particular day one of our Foden mixers was stopped and got a GV9 with immediate effect, because of, among other things, a broken spring. We were desperate for a mixer for the next day as they were not something we could hire. There was another Foden mixer in the garage waiting for spares so we took the number plates off it and put them on to the one with the prohibition notice, we did, in fact, change the spring, and sent it out. In the afternoon, the traffic examiner appeared about something else altogether and, stupidly, we had put the number plates off the mixer which had been put off the road on to the one waiting for spares. The examiner spotted it right away and said, 'That is not the number plate for that vehicle. What is going on? Don't touch it until I come back.' He took off to the phone box just up the road. I immediately phoned the quarry and, by good luck, the truck had just come back in. I stopped them from loading it again, took the plates off the one at the garage and sent my brother post haste over to the quarry with the number plates. He swapped them over and when he came back I put them into a pail with acid which we used to remove concrete. I believe the police were chasing about all the roads near the quarry looking for the mixer with the wrong number plates. Eventually, they went to the quarry and found the mixer which, by this time, had the proper plates. They then turned up at Garmouth with the traffic examiner, but it was his word against mine. They asked where the number plates off the truck in the garage were so I showed them the pail. Then they asked how we got the mixer over to the quarry. I said we had used trade plates. I knew that they didn't believe me but they couldn't prove anything. We did this quite a lot as we always had a couple of spare trucks without a licence. Our fleet was mainly made up of Dodge trucks and if one of them broke down we just swapped the plates. After this sham ally with the mixer we had to change the chassis plates as well because police stopped a few of our trucks and checked the number plate with the chassis plate. A few weeks later I got word to appear in front of the traffic commissioners in Aberdeen.

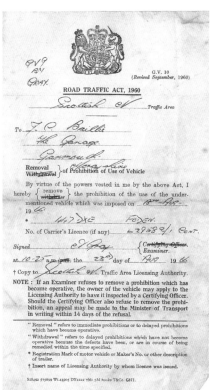

Copy of GV9 Prohibition for the Foden Mixer.

I didn't have to appear as, at the time, I was often sick which was eventually diagnosed as a stomach ulcer and the worry of appearing in front of the traffic commissioners aggravated it. In my absence they suspended two of our licences for, I think, three months, which didn't make a lot of difference as I had four spare licences which were actually on scrapped trucks so I just transferred them on to the suspended trucks. There was a write up in the daily paper. The headline said, 'Commissioner says, 'I don't know how this man can sleep in his bed at night.'

Another good contract we picked up was for William Tawse, public works contractors in Aberdeen. They had an office in Elgin and one in Inverness. The Elgin branch was already a good customer of ours but only for an odd truck now and again. Then we got the chance to quote for all their haulage needs for up to ten trucks for about a year on the A9 Dalmagarry to Bogbain dual carriageway, an eight mile stretch of road. Our bid was accepted and the job started on 28/3/1977, with five trucks building up to about twelve. We had to buy a lot more trucks because we still had our existing customers to keep happy. Initially we depended quite a lot on hiring drivers from around Inverness and appointed James Branson in charge. That didn't work as we used to pay our staff on a Thursday and half of them wouldn't appear on Friday. We started paying them on the Friday but then, of course, if we needed drivers on Saturday, as we quite often did, they weren't available. I went and bought some cheap caravans and set up a camp on the site with men from the Elgin area which was a great success. James Branson's job was to keep the trucks running and look after all the paperwork. He was told that as long as he kept the trucks moving and the paperwork up to date he could just sit down and read a newspaper, or whatever. I don't think he did get a lot of time to himself as he made a first class job. I don't think anyone else would have done as well. I went up there once and asked where Jimmy was. One of the drivers said a truck had broken down just up the road a bit. I went to have a look and there he was, lying in about six inches of mud, underneath a Dodge, fitting new bolts to the prop shaft.

Another time I found Jimmy in his caravan with a Foden gear box lying on his bed all in pieces. He had put down a ground sheet first.

That was Jimmy, a really first class employee and I cannot speak highly enough of him. When we first employed Jimmy someone said to me that I would rue the day as he was a rough character. In reality it was the firm he was working for that was rough and they were wrong about him. He wasn't the only one, we had a very good bunch of employees and they contributed a lot to the success of Baillie Brothers. When interviewing men for driving jobs I always gave preference to ex farm servants or, at least, someone brought up in the country as opposed to anyone brought up in any of the larger towns. Of course, back then there wasn't such a thing as a heavy goods drivers licence, a car licence was all that was needed.

After the Dalmagarry to Bogbain stretch of road was finished Tawse then landed the contract for a six mile dual carriageway stretch on the A9 between Aviemore and Kingussie. Once again we were awarded the contract for all their haulage needs and again we set up camp on the site with Jimmy Branson in charge. Another profitable job.

An episode I would like to forget was with a boy I had employed when I was in the fire wood business. He had just left school and would have been about sixteen, a first class worker. He stayed with us until he was eighteen then went into the army and was stationed at Fort George. He was only in about six weeks when he and another soldier absconded. He didn't go home to his mother but came to us in Garmouth. He still had his uniform on and had torn his kilt jumping a fence. My wife got him to take it off while she repaired it and we talked him into going back to Fort George. He agreed to do this, although he had no money, so we gave him enough for his bus fare. About twenty years passed before we saw him again. He had left the army with catering skills and had spent some time working on cruise ships. He was now living in Dufftown and wanted to buy a pub. He didn't have enough money so he asked us to finance him. I talked him out of the pub business and suggested he go for a cafe that was for sale instead. I knew that he had a bit of a drink problem but had no idea he was an alcoholic. We employed three of a staff and I appointed one of the girls as assistant manager. Well, every other day she would phone me about his antics. The cafe was licensed so, of course, alcohol was there for the taking. We did our stock-taking and there was quite a discrepancy so I ripped him up for that. We were also losing customers because of his being drunk on the premises. The final straw came when the girl phoned to tell me that he had arrived drunk around 8.30pm and ordered all the customers out. I left it until the morning and, just in case there was any trouble, my brother Gordon came with me. In fact there was no trouble, he was told to remove any personal belongings from the premises, give us the keys and not set foot in the cafe ever again. If he tried to do so for whatever reason, the under manager was told to phone the police. He got all this in writing. As far as I know he was not a drinker when he went into the army but after about twenty years he came out an alcoholic.

We tried running the place ourselves with the girl appointed as under manager in full charge but by this time the place had such a bad name it was a losing battle. We put the place up for sale and actually didn't lose that much as we got a bit more than we paid.

The next story, although horrendous at the time, on looking back, I wouldn't have liked to have missed. My daughter, Ann, as well as being transport manager, also did the sign-writing on our trucks but as our fleet increased she didn't have time. We had to look for someone else. All our tyres were bought from a firm in Buckie, Northern Oils, owned by Mr. Martin Reid. He told me about a Polish chap, Edward Jablonski, living in Whitehills, near Banff, a freelance sign-writer. Mr. Reid said he would contact him and ask him to get in touch with me. Edward said he could start next morning. I had a prior appointment so my brother showed him what had to be done. When I got back I went through to see how he was getting on. Of course, he didn't know who I was and, as usual, I had my dungarees on, so when we started a conversation he said, 'Do you work here?' I said, 'Yes.' He asked, 'Is this a good firm to work for?' I replied, 'Not that great. Bad payers. I hope you got paid before you started.' You should have seen his face, but after that we became the best of friends and I sub-contracted quite a lot of work to him.

He still had quite a few relations in Poland including his father who, at ninety, wasn't expected to survive another year. Edward wanted to go back to spend the Christmas holiday with his father and invited Doris and I to accompany him and his wife. We jumped at the chance. It was Christmas 1978, the arrangements were all made and flights booked but from the word go, everything that could go wrong did. First off, our visas and passports went missing in the post because of the Christmas rush. The travel agents arranged for us to go to the passport office in Glasgow where they would supply us with temporary ones. However, we were not going to be down there in time to collect them. They arranged for us to collect them the following morning, but the office didn't open until 9am and we had to be at the airport for 9.30am. The travel agents, very helpfully, organized someone to attend to us at 8am. Of course, it was the travel agent's fault as they hadn't allowed for the postal delays. After a pretty hectic time we reached the airport with very little time to spare. Edward didn't have this problem because, although he had been resident in Britain since the war some thirty years before, he never became nationalized, still had a Polish passport and didn't need a visa.

Before we left Doris and I had fallen out about something and were not on speaking terms but we set off for Whitehills where we were to pick up Chrissie and Edward. At Whitehills we were getting ready to leave, I thought everyone was in the car and moved off, then heard a yell. I had run over my wife's foot. Thinking I was still on top of her foot I reversed and ran over it again. She didn't say a word, but it must have been sore because when she took off her shoe her foot was all swollen.

We went on to Perth where Chrissie's son, Graham, lived. I was to leave my car at Perth and Graham would take us to Glasgow Airport where we had booked a hotel for the night. We landed safely at Warsaw Airport and were faced with five gates checking our documents, all with a long queue. We joined the end of one and after about an hour and a quarter we were nearly there with only four people in front when the attendant said her time was up and shut the gate. We had no hope but to join another queue which was just as long as the first one. Chrissie tried to argue with her but to no avail. When we finally got through we were met by Edward's sister Marilia. We took a train to Gdansk and then a bus to Jastarnia where we would be staying with another of Edward's sisters, Yolla, and her husband Yan. He had been a fisherman, now retired. He had, apparently, been drunk at one time and had foul mouthed the communist party. Unluckily he had been within earshot of some secret policemen. He was arrested, charged and sent to jail for one year for what they called 're-training'. They also confiscated his boat, leaving him and his family more or less destitute. There was another sister, Agnes, her husband had also been a fisherman with his own boat but now also retired. Agnes had been taken away as slave labour by the Germans during their occupation. They had subjected her to some experiments which resulted in her being unable to have children. She had some horrendous stories to tell. She felt that she had been lucky besides some other women detained by the Germans. Jastarnia was just a small fishing village with about five fishing boats based there, all privately owned. The catch all had to be sold to the government at their price, the fishermen were not even allowed to take any home for their own consumption. I believe quite a few had been caught and, depending on how much they had taken, given varying lengths of time in jail.

This was our first night staying with Yolla and at bed time we were shown our room. We got ready for bed which consisted of just a wooden frame with slats. We weren't long in bed when the damned thing collapsed, so we ended up sleeping on the floor. Next day we went for a walk around the town. One thing surprised me, we went into a supermarket, every bit as big as the supermarkets here but with absolutely nothing in them except for mountains of butter. Nobody seemed to know why there was so much butter and literally nothing else. There were other shops owned by the government where you could buy just about anything but the only currency they would accept was American dollars. Edward had told us to exchange our sterling for dollars before we left home.

It was pretty cold especially at night, which was to be expected as this was the second week in December. Into our second week the frost got so severe we watched boats coming into the harbour with the railings, which would have been made from tubular pipes about four inches in diameter, coated with up to a foot of ice. The ropes were also covered. In fact, ice had formed all over. I think if they had stayed out any longer the weight of ice would have sunk them. Worse was to come. In the morning the waves were frozen and as far as we could see, were hundreds of swans frozen in the water, all dead. This was the worst frost in Poland for forty years. When out in the town you had to keep moving, if you stopped you could feel the frost creeping up from the soles of your feet. It lasted right through Christmas and into the New Year although the second week wasn't quite as bad. But we managed to have a good time what with parties at friends homes and plenty vodka. When we arrived there, we were wakened every morning by the crowing of cockerels but on Christmas Day, total silence. The cockerels were all in the pot.

One thing I didn't like much was the outside dry toilets. Where we stayed they were in the garden about thirty metres from the house. We had to be pretty desperate before we ventured out. When you got there the hoosie was full of snow, the seat was covered in ice and, just as I remembered from my school days, the toilet paper was old newspapers

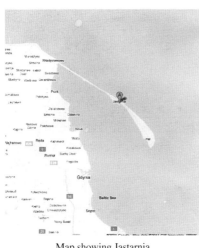

Map showing Jastarnia.

This is the small fishing village of Jastarnia where we stayed. It is about seven miles out into the Baltic sea. At the far point about three miles away is a place called Hel. Nobody was allowed to enter as it was a military zone. Although the strip of land looks just like a road at its narrowest it is actually about two miles wide.

The drinking water was pumped up from wells deep underground but because the strip of land was so narrow the water was salty. Every household had a holding tank so that some of the salt collected at the bottom and the water overflowed into another tank connected to the tap The water still tasted salty though so it was obviously just water which had seeped through from the Baltic.

To the south of Jastarnia is a wooded area four or five miles square where, according to the locals, a German battalion of some five thousand men had been trapped by the Russians when they had invaded Poland The Russians did not go in and kill or capture the Germans, they had the place surrounded and left them to starve.

There was not a cat, dog, horse or rat of any description left in that area when they finally surrendered. They were then shot. A sad story, although understandable as the Germans, by all accounts committed atrocities when they invaded Russia.

Now it was getting near time for us to go home. In the last couple of days there had been a large amount of snow and wind and many roads were impassable. We had to get to Gdynia, a distance of about thirty miles to catch the train back to Warsaw. We were told that the buses were running so we went to the bus stop but every one that came was full to the point where people were crammed in like sardines. One man had only managed to get one leg in, the other was dangling in mid air and he was desperately hanging on with both hands.

Marilia went to see if we could get a taxi. She didn't get a taxi but found someone she knew to take us to Gdynia. Off we set, but he was short of petrol and the petrol stations were few and far between. One we tried had run out, so were stuck again and it was freezing cold. Some Polish soldiers were clearing snow off the roads and our car driver said if we gave him some dollars he would go and see if he could buy some petrol. We gave him a handful of dollars and away he went. About twenty minutes later he came back with a jerry can full of petrol and set about to pour it into his tank. He then discovered that his radiator had burst with the frost. I may say that it wasn't possible to buy anti-freeze, it was all reserved for the military. So that was us stuck again. We had no choice but to go to the nearest bus stop and hope to get on one, which we eventually did. I think we were just lucky as a few people had just got off. We eventually made it to the railway station at Gdynia where we were to catch the overnight sleeper to Warsaw. We were all pretty tired by this time as it had taken us a whole day to travel thirty miles.

We had about an hour to wait for the train. There was one about every hour and they were running late because of the bad weather. We all went to the wash rooms to have a good wash. The ladies had started to strip off their top clothes when they looked in the mirror and they could see us. The clothes went back on quick. We didn't see them, I don't know why, maybe we didn't look in the right mirror. We didn't know about this until they told us after. It must have all been done by mirrors and what for I don't know.

Another thing that never ceased to amuse me was that all the public toilets had an attendant, usually ladies in later life, about sixty-five to seventy. When you went in you had to give them one schlotti, which was like a halfpenny in sterling and she handed you a piece of paper about eight inches square.

We eventually got on the train, there was no heating, it was absolutely freezing so instead of taking our clothes off we crawled under the blankets with our clothes on and the train set off. About an hour into the journey the heating came on and we were then just about melted. It was like that all night. Obviously the frost must have damaged the thermostat. We didn't get much sleep. We arrived in Warsaw late morning and set off to go to the house of a friend of Marilia's where we were going to stay for a few days. We set off walking which was a nightmare as the thaw had set in and the pavements were covered in slush with bits of hard snow underneath, very hard to walk on. Marilia took the lead and I can only describe her as a mountain goat. We couldn't keep up with her. Chrissie kept saying to Edward, 'Tell your sister to slow down, tell her to f---g slow down.' We were just in fits of laughter. Of course, Edward, who had a lung disease didn't have enough breath to tell his sister or to answer Chrissie. The final straw for us was when we heard Chrissie muttering, 'I will be more in need of a f----g holiday when I get home.' But it was really hard going. We passed a cafe and Marilia asked if anyone would like coffee. Chrissie said, 'Thank God for that.'

In Poland, whenever you went in to a cafe, or in fact any public place, everyone had to hand over their coat and, I think, handbag as well, but Chrissie being in such a temper went marching in, straight to the back of the cafe and sat down. We were at the desk and Doris, who was prone to unstoppable laughter was in hysterics. I couldn't see what she was laughing at. She just pointed to the back of the cafe and there was Chrissie with an attendant waving her arms about. Of course, Chrissie hadn't a clue what she was on about. Edward got it all sorted out and we finished our coffee and set off again. We then came to a street where all the houses were exactly the same, all had concrete outside stairs. We came to one house and Marila said, 'This is the one.' She and Edward would go up to make sure that the lady was at home. When they got to the top of the steps Marilia discovered it was the wrong house. Edward was carrying a large case, the idea being that he would not have to go up the steps twice. Well, when she said that it was the wrong house, he nearly had a fit. I learned some new swear words and some Polish ones as well that day. At last we found the right house, but Edward made Marilia go up first and he stayed at the bottom until we got confirmation that it was the right one.

We still had three days to go before our flights so we got to look round Warsaw. Most of the city had been destroyed in the war but one whole street had been completely rebuilt as it had been before the war. They started by advertising for any pre-war photographs and received hundreds of images from which they copied the buildings.

Time was now up so we made our way to the airport. We had to go through Polish customs and they were pretty rough. They emptied all our cases looking for any gold or silver jewellery which had originated in Poland and also currency, especially dollars or sterling. You were allowed to take as much cash as you liked in to Poland but you were not allowed to take any out. We knew this as Edward had been caught once before. On the same flight was a friend of Edward's, also Polish, but now living in Aberchirder in Aberdeenshire. He had a gold ring and asked my wife if she would take it through for him. She agreed to this and put it into her handbag. Sure enough, we were stopped and a lady emptied our cases out onto the table. She then started to rummage about in my wife's handbag and found about one hundred pounds in Scottish bank notes. She held up the notes and said, 'Currency.' My wife argued with her and said, 'No currency.' The lady shouted to a man to come and look. He obviously had never seen Scottish notes before and he and the lady argued back and forth. He must have said to let it go, so she threw the money into the handbag and threw the bag down among the contents of the cases.

Because of her finding the money she didn't find the ring. They weren't finished yet though. They took Doris to a cubicle and strip searched her. We were left to repack the cases. There is no doubt in my mind that someone had seen her being given the ring, but of course they didn't find anything. She was extremely lucky.

We were glad to get into the departure area and within half an hour we were on the plane and heading for home. I would never like to repeat this experience but it was one I wouldn't have missed for anything because, in spite of everything, we had some great laughs.

This is Edward Jablonski with a doll's house built with a fret saw, a toffee hammer and glue. This was his hobby when he retired. He made a lot of things, this was the most ambitious. When it was finished he raffled it, the money going to charity.

In 1989 we got the chance to go back to Poland again with Edward and Chrissie. In the summer this time and with my car, a Ford Fiesta Diesel, which I had bought new just five weeks before. This way we could see a bit more of Poland. We were booked to go on a Polish container ship leaving from Middlesborough. There was only space for five cars when we arrived and we were told

Edward was a first class painter. This is an ice cream van painted for a chap in Elgin.

to leave our car. We were showed to our cabins and told that they would give us a shout when they were ready to load the cars. In the meantime we were taken to the cook house where we were given tea. We were told the times for breakfast, dinner and supper and after that, if we wanted a snack, we just had to go down to the kitchen and help ourselves. After about half an hour we got a shout that they were ready to load so Edward and I went to the lift which would take us down to the cars. Halfway down the lift stuck. We were panicking in case our car was left behind. There was a telephone kind of apparatus but it didn't seem to be working, Edward was shouting but nobody seemed to hear him. I eventually gave the door an ill-tempered rattle and away it went. The problem was that the door had not been properly shut.

Two days later we arrived in Gdansk and hit our first problem. The Polish officials said there was something wrong with Edward's documents. He was taken into an office where they said he would most likely be held for some time but, if he had some dollars to give them, he would get through right away. It cost him thirty dollars to pay off the corrupt officials, a problem we were to come up against frequently during our tour round Poland. They didn't tell Edward what the 'problem' was with his papers.

We duly set off for Jastarnia, a distance of about sixty miles which we reached without any mishaps. We stayed there for a few days with Edward's sister before we went touring. Our intention was to stay in bed and breakfast or hotels on the way. By the second day we were in need of fuel. The filling stations either had long queues or signs saying, 'Sorry, no fuel.' We joined the end of a long queue, of about forty cars. When we got down to about seven, the attendant shut the station saying the tanks were empty. Some of the people waiting created quite a disturbance but eventually, they all disappeared. Edward then went to the attendant and said that we had dollars if he could give us fuel. As soon as he mentioned dollars the man said, 'Pull your car in.' He filled the tank with as much as it would take and Edward gave him twenty dollars, which I'm sure went straight into his own pocket as the filling stations were all owned by the Communist Government.

We stopped that night at a hotel in Bydgoszcs. In the morning we went to the dining room for breakfast. I can't remember what we had for breakfast but I recall there was a plate on the table with slices of bread. Doris picked up a slice intending to spread it with butter. The slice underneath had unmistakable toothmarks where someone had taken a bite out of it. That put us off breakfast. Edward did complain to the waitress but she just shrugged her shoulders and went to get more bread. We didn't wait and went to the office to pay our dues.

Edward still had a Polish passport and needed to go to Warsaw so he could arrange a visa to return to Britain. We had just reached the outskirts of a small town called Plock and had joined a line of traffic, all at the same speed, when a policeman signalled for us to stop. He had obviously noticed the British number plates and accused us of speeding. He asked Edward, the driver, for his documents. He then said, 'I could let this drop if you were to hand me some dollars.' That cost us another twenty dollars into the pocket of the policeman.

Edward went to the British Consul in Warsaw to get his visa but returned empty handed because he couldn't prove who he was. I had to go and vouch for him. Even then, they were a bit reluctant to issue the visa. We were there for about an hour and a half. They asked me a lot of questions. We were left sitting in a room. I expect they would have been doing a bit of phoning to check I was telling the truth. Anyway, Edward eventually got his visa.

The next place we stayed was Temobrze. We were shown to our room but behind the door was a big waste bucket, overflowing, full of flies and smelling awful. It was absolutely disgusting. Edward contacted the man in charge and he gave us another room. It seemed to be clean enough but when we went through to the bathroom someone had stolen the wash hand basin, it had been torn off the wall and the water pipes flattened and bent over. The bed was clean enough, though, so we decided we would manage to do without the sink. We just went to Edward and Chrissie's room for a wash. It was the holiday period so all the best hotels were booked and the ones we landed in were mostly all state run and none of the workers seemed to give a damn.

Our next stop was at a place called Nowa Huta. It is not shown on the map, I think it is part of Krakow. We stayed there with a couple who did bed and breakfast and I must say it was one of the best places we had stayed in. They told us they hadn't seen the sun for about sixty years because of the pollution caused by the many factories in the area. We had noticed the smell when we arrived. Apparently a lot of the people living and working there had respiratory problems and the death rate from lung disease was very high. One of the main reasons for us coming to Krakov was to visit the Wieliczka salt mines to see the carvings made by prisoners working in the mines over hundreds of years. Our hosts told us that it had been closed for renovation for about a year so we had to forget about that. After that, though, everything went accordingly to plan.

top left: Map of Poland with a rough estimate of the route we took. I have shown the main roads on the map but we quite often used second class roads which were more interesting. top right: Doris and I in front of one of the hotels we stayed in. bottom left: Doris and Chrissie on the boat. bottom right: We stopped for a snack away off the main road.

We stayed at Edward's sister's house.

There were 400 containers on the ship.

We eventually landed back at Jastarnia. Edward wanted to visit someone he had been at school with so off he went by himself. After the visit he left to come home but found the battery was flat. He had to borrow a battery charger which he left attached to the car for about an hour. That allowed him to get it started but a couple of days later it went flat again. I had a look at it and found the bolt which attached the earth wire to the bell housing had never been tightened. I tightened it and had no more bother with the battery going flat. This seemed to fix a problem I had with the temperature gauge as well.

It was now time to go to Gdansk to catch the boat for home which we did with no mishaps. This time the boat went through the Keil Canal as they had containers for Tillbury docks up the River Thames. When the boat docked the customs officials came aboard and searched the cars. They weren't very thorough and didn't search our luggage. After unloading, the boat then set sail for Middlesborough where our car was unloaded and we set off for home. A really enjoyable holiday.

In 1984, I was fifty six, I went to the doctor as I had been having pains in my arms, especially after any exertion. I went to see a specialist and heard nothing for about three weeks. I then got a phone call to go and see my GP right away. The first thing he said to me was, 'You had better go home and get all your affairs in order.' I thought that meant I didn't have long to go. I asked the doctor and he said, 'How do I know?' I was put on medication for my heart, which was the problem, and he said I should give up the Managing Director role and stay on in an advisory capacity only. After I got home and had a talk with Doris, we decided I should retire altogether and at least get maybe a couple of years of retirement. I am now eighty-four years old and my heart has never bothered me again after I started the medication. The doctor, however, about the same age as me, died of a heart attack about twenty years ago. I probably didn't really have to retire so early but then, if I had carried on there might have been an adverse effect. We'll never know.

The first thing I did after retiring was to book flights to Canada. I had been thinking about going there for a while and just hadn't got round to it. I thought we should go as long as I was fit enough. My father David and my uncle James were identical twins. James went to Canada to work with William Thompson, a cousin. He was an agricultural contractor with seven children. Sadly, William took ill and died shortly after James went to work with him. James kept the business going for William's widow and eventually married her. They also went on to have seven children making a total of fourteen which gives you an idea of how many relations I have in Canada. About fifty six, I believe. I managed to meet quite a lot of them and they were all very good to us. They took turns taking days off work to show us around. They asked what my interests were. I said vintage trucks, barn engines and steamers of which I already had quite a collection. In Canada there was a lot of vintage machinery in museums and also still lying about on farms. I got a bit more than I bargained for, every day we visited a different museum, but I enjoyed it and so did Doris who was very much into vintage stuff as well.

Just some of the John Deere tractors this family saved over the years. (below middle left) The present day farmer standing beside the John Deere which is his current tractor. He has every John Deere owned by his family since the 1920's. Every time they bought a new John Deere the old one was kept. They were lying about all over the place and, unlike Britain where we are never more than about fifty miles from the sea, there is very little rust and most of the tractors were in fairly good condition.

More vintage vehicles seen in Canada. (bottom right) Nodding Donkey, they were scattered all over Alberta and used for pumping oil from wells.

The last thing I organized before retiring was a two way radio system owned by a man called Brian Casey. He also owned a shop and Post Office in Urquhart. He had four repeater stations, one on the Black Isle, one in Grantown on Spey, one in Elgin and one at Gardenstown, near Macduff. These gave good coverage of the north east and were a great asset for the haulage business. I wish I'd had it years before About a year later he had a cash flow problem and approached me to see if I wanted to buy the communications side of his business. I was very much interested but thought it only right to approach my brother Gordon who was now in charge of Baillie Brothers. He said no, that he had enough on his mind without any more to think about. I decided to buy it myself. Mr. Casey wanted £6,500 for the business, I offered £5,000 which he accepted. I approached my three daughters, Jane Birnie, Ann Morrison, Brenda MacBain and my son William and they all put £500.00 into the business, I put in the rest. We took possession on the first of May, 1983. The whole system was in need of an overhaul which we proceeded to implement. First we had to get a better site for the mast in Elgin as, being situated in the town, it was too low resulting in poor coverage. I went to see Mr. Christie, the owner of the Blackhills estate and managed to rent a site at the top of the Tienland hill where I put up a temporary twelve foot mast. We overcame the problem of no electricity supply by installing a twenty four volt wind charger and batteries which worked quite well.

My intention was to erect a one hundred foot mast later on. We applied for planning permission which was granted without any problem. I had three twenty foot mast sections which I had found up at the Black Isle repeater station left over when they had erected a new mast at some time. I set to and built another two twenty foot sections. The ground at the Tienland was moss so I got four fifty gallon oil drums and filled them with concrete. I cemented in lorry half shafts with a ring welded on to the part that was protruding to hold the guide ropes and then buried them in the ground, one at each corner. We had a bit of a mishap when we were erecting them. Erecting the mast at the Tienland hill near Elgin. We couldn't get a crane up to that site so we used tractors. It looks a bit twisted in the photographs but once it was up and the guide ropes on it straightened up.

We eventually succeeded and that just left the mast at Gardenstown which also needed replacing. I sent off for a brochure of new mast sections but they were all very expensive. Looking at the photographs I could see that all I needed to make them was the steel and a welder which I had. I bought the materials and set about building them. I

ised the same specifications as the brochure and built five twenty foot
sections, much more cheaply than the prices quoted.

We now had to erect the two of them. That was a fair job in itself but
we eventually succeeded.

(above)The crane with a 110 ft jib getting ready to lift the
sections. (bottom left) My son William, and my son in law John
Birnie bolting the sections together. Note, no safety harness, but
no safety inspectors to be seen either. This was at Gardenstown.

We kept this business for three years then
sold out to Dick Boyd Communications
for a substantial profit at the end of
November, 1986.

Baillie Brothers was still going well. My brother Gordon had taken
over when I retired and got in tow with an engineer called Jerry Job. He
had worked with Tulloch of Nairn but had a disagreement with Tulloch
and was now out of a job. He had been a very good customer of ours,
hiring trucks regularly from us. He had been the man in charge of the
Tulloch operations at Ardesier which was connected to the North Sea Oil
Operations, building and repairing oil rigs. In 1988 he had a proposition
for Gordon and himself to go into partnership and start a public works
business. They agreed to go ahead with it and the company was to be
called Job Construction. It did very well completing a lot of profitable
public works jobs which Jerry had been successful in tendering for.

They accumulated quite a reserve of working capital. Then in 1992 Jerry Job decided that he would like to go it alone and offered to buy our Baillie Brothers share. Gordon declined and instead bought out Jerry Job's share changing the firm's name to Linkwood Construction. In hindsight that was a bad move because after Jerry left things started to go wrong. Gordon employed an engineer to be in charge but he turned out to be a complete disaster. Gordon dispensed with his services in 1993 and replaced him with another manager who was pretty good at his job but had a struggle with the debts accumulated by his predecessor. He was gradually reducing the debts until he took on a road job in Skye. This was a section of the approach road for the new bridge linking Skye with the mainland. The job was sub-contracted from Balfour and Beatty. The contract had stated that any rock on the site had to be allowed for. We don't know if the manager missed that or not but when we started excavating we came upon a seam of rock which he thought we could claim 'extras' for. When he realized the contract stated there would be no extras for rock he then said it was a seam of 'rotten rock' which could be ripped using a big D9 Caterpillar transported up from Glasgow. Of course the rock was not rotten and when they tried to rip it they broke the ripper which cost us £25,000. We ended up having to blast the seam which cost a fortune. The next mishap, which might not have been entirely his fault, came about when they used a stockpile of material left over from another stretch of road by another contractor for infill. The council engineer condemned it and it all had to be removed. We were just very unlucky as the other firm had used it and got away with it. The manager still insisted that we would eventually get this money back but the firm was being propped up by the other two firms Baillie Brothers and Linkwood Truck Sales. The result being they also had a large overdraft, although still solvent. The same could not be said about Linkwood Construction. Then the bank finally gave up on us.

All this worry had taken its toll on my brother's health and he decided to retire. My eldest son John Baillie then took over. The first thing he did was to make the manager redundant and put Linkwood Construction into liquidation. He sold all the plant and made sure that all money due to third parties was paid, all except the tax man. He then had to start and try to build up the other two companies which he succeeded in doing, although it was touch and go. The fact that the haulage and garage side of the business was very busy helped.

By this time we had moved to a new garage which we had built at Linkwood Industrial Estate, Elgin at a cost of over £9,000,000. It was at that time the largest and most well equipped commercial vehicle repair centre north of Aberdeen, all devised and planned by my brother Gordon. We were now main agents for Foden, Renault, Suzuki and Hino.

This is the new garage which we built at Linkwood Industrial Estate.

Quite early on in the business I devised a pay structure of my own. All the drivers got a maintenance bonus of ten shillings which could be stopped if their vehicle was not maintained properly. In practice, I think I only had to stop the bonus about twice. I also introduced a service bonus of two shillings and sixpence per week for every year a driver was with us. By this time some of the men had been with us for five or six years, so it did make a difference to their pay at the end of the week. It also helped if a new employee had started agitating about pay or conditions as the others didn't want to lose their bonus by joining in the complaints. It doesn't seem like a lot of money but the average wage was about twenty five pounds a week so the bonuses were useful.

In the late seventies there was a nationwide transport strike. Our employees didn't want to strike but I could see they were in a difficult position, there were pickets all over the place. I decided to pay them all off so they could draw unemployment benefit. They were then pestered by the union to join. One of the drivers went round them all and got quite a few to join. They had to pay a fee every week so that didn't last long as he had a lot of trouble trying to get the money from them. In the end he gave up the union then phoned me to see if I would be prepared to collect the money off their weekly wage packet. I just said no, so that was the end of that.

In 1974 I decided I would arrange a dinner dance for all the employees. My wife organized it all and booked the hotel and the band. We were members of the British Legion and went to different branches most weekends where they had a band. Doris was able to pick the best of the bands. We usually had to book them about a year in advance. The first dance was held on 8/11/74 at the St. Andrews Hotel, Lhanbryde. It was a great success and we went on to enjoy a dinner dance every year. At that time we had about fifty employees. Everything was free for them and a partner, if they wanted to take friends they could but they would have to be paid for.

The first staff dance. (top left) The employees presented the ladies with flowers. Front row from left, our mother, my wife, Doris, and Gordon's wife, Pat. (top right) Another staff dance photograph. (bottom left) This photo is of a presentation of a mug to Brian Marnoch, something I started doing after he completed twelve years with Baillie Brothers. In fact, Brian stayed with the firm and retired in 2009 having been with the firm for forty eight years. (bottom right) Left to right, David Baillie, our mother, Jane Baillie, Doris Baillie, myself, John Baillie, Pat Baillie and Gordon Baillie

Something else I did was to arrange an annual bus run and meal for old age pensioners from Kingston and Garmouth. The late Janet Marnoch, was in charge of the amenities at that time and she arranged it all for me. I asked her not to say who had paid for the outing and I don't know if the pensioners ever knew where the money came from. I suspect they did but it would be thirty-five years ago so I don't think any of them would still be on the go now. Some of the younger villagers would probably remember because there must have been speculation as to who was the mystery donor.

About 1976 I bought a Bedford Camper Van and Doris and I went away most weekends. We were always on the look out for old derelict trucks or barn engines. The give away for a barn engine would be a chimney sticking out of the side of a barn or shed. By this time barn engines were mostly redundant as threshers and bruisers were being driven by tractors. We went across to the Orkneys for the first time ever with the camper. My brother in law, John MacKinnes and his wife, also had a camper van and they came with us. The timing belt broke on my camper so John towed us to a small garage in a village called Holm. The owner said, 'Just drive her into that shed and I will be with you as soon as I fix this garden mower.' This would have been about 10am. He re-appeared about noon and said, 'Come into the house, my wife has made a meal for you.' After the meal he made no move to start working again. By this time I was looking upon him as a friend and as he hadn't managed to fix the mower I asked if I could borrow some tools and start taking off the camper's front grill. He replied, 'Yes, just help yourself.' Of course, he had to send to Inverness for a belt which was due to arrive on the ferry the following morning. It took until about five pm to get the mower going and when the owner came to collect it he charged £2.50. I just could not believe it, that was a whole day's work. But that is the Orcadian nature, so laid back, what great people. In fact I did all the work on the camper myself when we got the new belt, the only thing he did was to set the timing.

I eventually changed the Bedford for a Mercedes diesel camper and we went back to visit him the next time we went to Orkney. He had a petrol pump on the forecourt at his garage but I asked if he had diesel. He said, 'Just reverse round the back.' I thought he might have a pump, but no, I could not believe my eyes. He produced a gallon jug, all stamped by the customs, stuck a filler into my tank and proceeded to use it to take diesel out of a tank set up on blocks. He filled up my tank with eight gallons. He then said, 'I'm just going for a cup of tea. Would you like a cup?' What a cracker of a man, but I don't think he was destined to be rich money-wise, but rich in every other respect.

I had another laugh when visiting a friend in Orkney. I was standing talking to him when a neighbour came along and said, 'I see some of your cattle have broken out, they're eating all your winter feed.' His reply was, 'Ach well, what they eat today they won't get in the winter.'

After I retired I had a lot more time for my hobby, restoring antique trucks, tractors and barn engines. My main interest was the old barn engines, I had more than a hundred of these having picked them up very cheaply, more or less scrap value. I took a lot of them home from Orkney. A friend, John Mackie, had a haulage business in Orkney and took loads to and from the mainland on a regular basis. He would transport them home for me.

By this time I had bought another camper van, a Mercedes diesel fitted with a tow bar. I had looked at one at the Glasgow Motor Show and had been very impressed with it. Not long after that one appeared in the Commercial Motor magazine. It was near Liverpool at a garage called Toronto Motors. I phoned them and discovered that it had been the personal property of the garage owner and was only a year and a half old. He had taken on a franchise agency for a make of car and had to sell the camper to finance it. I asked if he would take the Bedford in part exchange and he said yes. He asked me for some details and gave me a valuation there and then subject to seeing it. Every fifty miles or so the Bedford would hotter to a stop with petrol problems. This meant dismantling the carburettor and cleaning it. It had bothered me for a while and I had dismantled the whole petrol system, including cleaning out the petrol tank but never got to the bottom of it. It was a bit of a worry going to Liverpool, my worst fear was going through the Mersey Tunnel but my luck held and we made it. There was no quibble with the garage owner. He was a very nice chap and took Doris and I in for a meal. I thought I was back in Orkney.

We went to vintage rallies all over the UK including the Thousand Engine Rally at Longleat, the Marquis of Bath's estate. We had a great time and were also allowed into the wildlife park. This rally was for barn engines only. We met some very interesting people and saw some very rare engines.

The Bedford

This is me at Longleat with quite a rare engine called a Handyman.

One of my favourite engines, a Crossley Lampstart.

The Mercedes

114

We visited many rallies, the Mearns, Banchory, Alford, Newbyth, Elgin, Dallas, Inverness, Alness, Dunrobin Castle and Halkirk. We had some great times and good laughs with some real characters always up to some trick or another. One time, at an Elgin rally, a man showed an engine driving a water pump which was circulating water from a barrel. Late in the evening, someone put a bottle of washing up liquid into the water. In the morning, within minutes of the owner starting it, the engine and the pump had disappeared under a mass of bubbles. Needless to say, the owner was not very happy but eventually saw the funny side of it.

There was a chap from Halkirk, the late John Begg, who always greeted everyone with, 'Would you like a fire distinguisher?' - a can of beer.

(far left) John Begg wiping the sweat off his pow. Probably pure beer.

(left) This is my Allan hot bulb engine. They were made in Aberdeen. As you can see I got First Prize.

I remember one time, on the way to Orkney, we went to visit John Begg. He said, 'We're having a party up at a nearby farm. You must come and we'll have a few fire distinguishers.' Doris and I said, 'OK.' I knew the farmer as he also went to rallies. I think his name was Sutherland but everyone called him Barnes, which was the name of his farm. There was a group of about eight folk at the farm when we arrived, mostly vintage collectors. I had never seen anything like it. There were gallons of whisky and it wasn't just strong, it was lethal. I was told afterwards it was home made. I wasn't told where, but that it was only made when there was a high wind so that it would disperse the smell. About one in the morning Barnes said, 'Would anyone like a fry up?' Everyone said, 'Yes.' At the back of the farm was the river Thurso. Barnes and another man went out for about twenty minutes and came back with a salmon, just out of the river. Out came the frying pan and the salmon was sliced with a hacksaw and fried. It tasted great.

By this time everyone was the worse for wear. John Begg was completely legless. They must have phoned for a taxi to take him home. The last I saw of him was two men carrying him off. We had the camper van so we made our way to bed. Next morning Barnes offered us breakfast but all I could take was a cup of tea. Doris had a good breakfast. Barnes was also pretty poorly so, after breakfast, his wife went out to attend to the cattle. She came back to say one of his cows had staggers, a disease in cattle which, if caught in time, can be cured. Barnes went out to give the cow an injection but his hand was shaking too much. His wife phoned for a neighbour to do it for him Never again. I suffered for days because of that illicit still. I often wonder if they still make it. I don't suppose so as most of the worthies from Halkirk are deceased. What a great crowd they were, just a laugh a minute.

Another character I often met at the rallies was Alistair MacIntosh, he was the employee of ours that nearly blew the factory at Dalcross to bits. He liked his dram. At a rally in Alford, his wife couldn't get the gas to light in their caravan. Alistair would crawl underneath to see what was wrong. In his drunken state he took the gas pipe from the cylinder and tried to blow through it. He was never coming out so Isobel, his wife, went to see what was going on. There he was with the gas pipe in his mouth, fast asleep. She shouted to me to help her pull him out, which I did. We got him into the caravan but he was a bit argumentative so I left him for about half an hour. I went to see if he was OK, Isobel said 'Look at him.' There he was, in his bed, not just under the blankets but under the mattress, sound asleep.

A local painter and decorator, Colin Smith *(The Fox)*, did some work for Alistair but never got paid. He went up every weekend to be paid but Alistair always had some excuse. Alistair decided he would put a stop to Colin pestering him and waited for him with a .22 rifle. As Colin approached Alistair aimed at a saw bench in the yard and fired when Colin was about three yards from it. The shot glanced off the side of the saw blade and gave Colin such a fright he never went back. He didn't get paid nor did he get the dust sheets he had left.

Colin The Fox

At Garmouth, 4 South Road,

That is Colin Smith's abode.

From the council it is rented

And DHSS is about demented.

No matter how they watch,

Colin they can not catch.

No matter what they try,

For them he is too fly.

BBC detector van is on its' rounds,

They're after Colin I'll be bound.

Many dodgers they are going to bust

And Colin, you can't see for dust.

If you are in need of a golf ball,

Lift the phone and give Colin a call.

Every day golfers on the course

Hit the ball with some force.

And there's another one for Colin.

No doubt he makes a fortune,

Through the golfer's misfortune.

In his house golf balls galore,

Sometimes he can't close the door.

At around four in the morning,

To the golf course he goes roaming.

Then back home he comes trudging

With balls his pockets are bulging.

The golfing men are all in a rage

And think Colin should be in a cage.

Says he, 'Man this is great fun,

I've got them all on the run.'

So golfers, if Colin you would fox,

Just leave the balls in their box.

Another time Alistair had been having bother with an infestation of rats. There was a shed built on to the side of the house and he had seen rats going along the top of the wall. He decided to have a crack at them and fixed a torch on to the shotgun. When he opened the shed door, sure enough, there was a rat running along the top of the wall. Alistair fired and immediately heard a scream. He went into the house to see what all the screaming was about and found Isobel, white as a ghost, with a bowl of trifle in her hands, full of lead pellets. A clock had also been shot off the wall. What Alistair didn't know was that the space between the top of the wall and the roof was only plasterboard.

By this time I had quite a collection of vintage engines and vehicles.

(far left) From left, Albion 1928, Bedford 1932, Albion 1935, in foreground Ferguson Tractor

(top right) A Ransomes Simms and Jeffreys Wizard Barn Engine

(middle left) Aveling Porter Steam Tractor 1922

(middle right) Foden 1950

(bottom left) Singer 1923

(bottom right) Austin 7, 1927

I got a phone call from a chap in Inverness to say that there was an engine in Skye which belonged to an estate. It had been driving a saw bench but, as they wanted to get rid of it, I could have it free if I took it away. I phoned the estate and was told to come and get it. I went over on the ferry, no bridge at that time, to see the engine. It had been removed from its foundations and was ready to lift. I had a tour around the island and came across two derelict Ferguson tractors, which I also acquired. I arranged to collect them the following Friday. A JCB was arranged to lift the engine on to the trailer. My son in law, John Birnie and a friend, David Murdoch, were going to follow the next day but they arrived that night. We were sheltering in an old quarry as it was an atrocious night with rain and high wind. Not unusual on the west coast of Scotland. By a stroke of luck they decided to shelter in the same quarry. We had just gone to bed at about eleven when there was a rattle at the camper door.

I thought it was the police as there was a sign saying, 'No overnight parking.' Then a voice shouted, 'Get the kettle on.' I realized who it was. By morning the weather had cleared up, the wind had died down so we set off to collect the engine. I had arranged for the digger to be there at nine-thirty but at eleven we were still waiting. I hung on until noon then went to where I had seen a JCB working on the road nearby. I asked the driver if he would come and load the engine for us. He said, 'Yes, no bother.' I set off back to where the engine was and met the JCB I ordered originally. I told him not to bother as I had someone else to do the job. He just turned about and set off home, not in the least bothered. The other JCB was on the way and reached about two hundred yards from us when there was a clatter from his engine. That was the end of that machine. I didn't know what to do then. My only hope was to try to get the original JCB but I wasn't sure what kind of reception I was going to get. Luckily, when I found him, he was quite unperturbed. He just jumped in his machine and turned it back. Firstly, he had to pull the broken down JCB out of the way and then loaded the engine on to the trailer without any trouble. Typical of the island people, nothing puts them up or down. After tying the engine on to the trailer we set off. We went about a hundred yards and the camper tow bar broke off, the trailer landed on the ground. The tow bar had been weakened by rust out of sight at the back. We had passed a garage on the way out so I went to see if they could weld it back on. The owner said they were so busy it would be Monday before they could fit us in. I said that I could weld it myself if he would let me use the equipment. He told me that would be no problem and to help myself. I set about and welded the tow bar and used some scrap angle iron to strengthen it. We hooked the trailer back on and set off.

The Ferguson Tractor.

This is the engine, a Lister Blackstone.

The Ferguson was loaded on to the other trailer with no problems, John and David towing it with the car. About a mile down the road the tow bar came adrift from the car. It had been borrowed from my nephew, Garry Baillie, as John's car didn't have a tow bar. We discovered it wasn't a proper tow bar but home made and bolted to the bottom of the boot. The four bolts had pulled out through the steel. We had to go back to the garage and get two lengths of scrap angle iron, drill holes to fit the holes in the boot of the car and bolted on the tow bar. That was a great success. They set off about fifteen minutes before us. About two miles down the road I came upon them sitting in a passing place with a puncture on the trailer. There was a car behind me and no room to pull in. I had to keep going until I found a lay-by and waited for them. They eventually appeared but the spare tyre they put on was a bit short of air. They had to go very slowly until they reached a garage a short distance down the road. The compressor was out of order so there was no choice but to carry on to the ferry and hope that the tyre held out until we reached the mainland, which it did. We found a garage, blew up the tyre and made it home with no more mishaps.

In 1991 a chap of about twenty-five came to my door. He said he was from Knoydart on the west coast and while he was visiting the north east on holiday, he was hoping to get some advice about an engine damaged by frost. It was a Ruston Diesel, installed in 1922 to drive a saw bench. All this time it never had anti freeze, nor the water drained in winter time and never had any trouble until the previous year, when they had a hard frost which was unusual in Knoydart. One or two people had directed him to me but I couldn't help him without seeing the damage. I decided I would go across and have a look, then I could advise him. He informed me that although Knoydart estate was on the mainland there was no road to reach it. We would have to park our camper at Mallaig and take the passenger boat. He said we would get accommodation in the estate house, plus all our food. This sounded like a good holiday for us so Doris and I set off the following week. We stayed that night in Mallaig and got the boat next morning.

The estate gave us a Land Rover to use all the time we were there. I then had a look at the damaged engine. They had removed the sleeve as the engine would have to be welded from the inside. The crack was at the bottom which was sitting on concrete. I told them that it would be a straightforward job if they could get a welder. They arranged to get someone but he didn't turn up so I offered to do the job for them. I needed welding kit which they had, and cast iron welding rods, which came by boat the next morning. While I was waiting for the rods, I machined the cracked casting with a small grinder, ready for welding. By this time the welder had been moved from their workshop, some distance away, to the engine house.

The welder was set for 440 volts and as the supply at the sawmill was only 220 volts I changed the setting on the welder to 220 volts but when I tried to weld, nothing happened. Apparently the 220 side was no longer working. They said they knew where they could borrow a welder, it would be on the next boat. It arrived on that afternoon's boat. I had never seen a welder like it, it was massive. I think it must have been one of the first ones invented. However, looks were deceiving, it turned out to be a very good welder. I was all set, I just sparked the welder once and blew the fuse in the wall. We tried another fuse but the same thing happened. I suggested fitting a stronger fuse but they wouldn't hear of it. Their electricity came from a hydro dam up in the hill and they were afraid we would damage the generator. We weren't stuck though. Up the road a bit someone had their own generator. It was a fair distance from the welder, so somebody went raking about the houses and borrowed about six extension cables.

I wasn't very impressed with this set up but got going with the welding. I hadn't been working long when someone came running in shouting that some of the extension cables were smoking. When I went to look, some of the cables were on fire so we couldn't use that set up. Another portable generator was brought over but it only had one and a half kilowatts and I said it wouldn't be any use. They were keen for me to try it as it produced enough power to light it's owners whole house, so I gave it a go, just to please them. As soon as I started there was a bang and that was the end of that. It was probably just a fuse but, as it was about four in the afternoon the chap said he had to go and would see what could be done in the morning. Doris and I went up to the big house where we were staying to get a bite to eat. We just had to help ourselves from the well stocked freezers and fridges so we didn't go hungry. After our meal I said to Doris that I was going back to have another go at welding the engine. She reminded me I had thought that if the fuse at the mains was replaced with a bolt it should work, so that was what I did. It worked a treat. I spent the next six hours on the job.

Welding cast iron is a slow job as you can only do about three millimetres at a time and then hammer it to take the strain out of the metal otherwise it would crack again. It then has to cool before you can go on to the next bit. I finished about 1.30 in the morning. The chap was over the moon when he came back. I had replaced the bolt with the original fuse. I advised him to get plastic metal to spread over the weld just in case there was seepage.

(top left) Engine with the sleeve removed, ready for welding. (top right) The casting showing the weld (middle left) The saw bench which the engine was driving. (middle right) The big house where we stayed (bottom left) The living room. (bottom right) The bathroom

Another funny thing happened at a vintage rally while I was having a blether with a spectator who had his dog with him on a lead. It was a very hot day and he mentioned that he thought the dog needed a drink. I said I had plenty of water in the camper and would give him some in a basin, which I did. The dog had just settled down to lap it up when an 8HP Petter two stroke gave out a loud bang. The dog got such a fright it tried to run off but couldn't because of the lead so ran round it's owner through between his legs, tying them together and then tripped him up so he landed on his back. After a few choice words, he got himself disentangled, stood up and got the dog quietened down.

As he was trying to coax his dog to drink again the engine gave another almighty bang, twice as loud as the first one. This time the dog really went berserk, ran round in a circle, tripped his master up again and he landed with his backside in the basin of water, lost hold of the lead and the dog took off doing about sixty miles per hour up through the field and disappeared among the trees. I never heard if he ever found the dog again. I expect he did. This happened at the Keith Rally in 1983.

The Petter that caused all the trouble.

This is a true story of an incident at Alistair MacIntosh's home in Orton. Alistair had his eye on an 8hp Petter engine thinking it would look good in his collection. The owner of the engine had done it all up and fitted it on a trolley. It was looking real braw when Alistair went to see it. Luckily the owner had taken a fancy to something smaller and Alistair had a small Crossley engine so they struck a deal. The engine was taken home and Alistair was standing in front of his shed admiring it, fair proud of his deal when his neighbour Ally Guthrie came across to see it. They decided to start it up.

Now, as anyone who has ever had anything to do with a two stroke Petter will know, if they are not set right, every time the governors cut in the silencer fills with gas and the next time it fires the gas explodes with a very loud bang. Alistair's engine started no problem and seemed to be running well when, all of a sudden, there was an almighty bang. The exhaust pipe shot up into the air, hit the lintel on top of the shed door, bounced off, thumped Ally on the head in passing and then clobbered a Ruston Hornsby engine situated just inside the shed breaking off the exhaust and silencer. To crown it all the Petter gave another tremendous bang, the trolley fell to pieces and the whole caboodle landed in a heap on the ground. Alistair was not at all amused, for that matter neither was Ally. Alistair, feeling sorry for himself, went into the house looking for sympathy from his wife, Isobel. Unfortunately, when she saw the heap of junk lying on the ground all she could do was laugh. In the end, the only solace that Alistair and Ally got was from a bottle of Johnny Walker which he had hidden in an old bruiser at the back of the shed. (Sorry for giving away your hidey-hole, Alistair, but that is the trouble with true stories, you have to tell the truth.)

How I lost part of my finger. I did a bit of woodwork when I had time, making bird feeding tables and nest boxes, or anything involving wood. I had a collection of model commercial vehicles and decided to make a rack to hold them.

When it was finished Doris said it would look better if the top was rounded instead of being just square. I agreed and went back out to my workshop to do the modification. In the process I cut the index finger off my left hand by the first joint with the circular saw. I tied a cloth round it and ran into the house.

Doris drove me to Elgin to A&E where they tidied it up. They must have wrapped the skin from my finger tip up over the top to close the wound and the nerves must have still been intact. This resulted in the feeling that when I touch anything with my finger tip it feels like the top of my finger. It was a very funny feeling but I've gradually become accustomed to it.

Here are some of the poems I wrote for the Spey Valley Vintage Club Newsletter.

This is the rack that caused all the trouble because of the rounded bit at the top.

The Worthies

Noo that winter's nearly past
The rally season comin' up fast.
Davie Murdoch working on his Shank's
Nae doot thinking up a few pranks.
The morn he's off tae hiv a rake aboot
He's heard o' a shed wi' a lum stickin' oot.
He'll maybe ging tae Tomintoul
For up there somewhere is a Powell.
There is nae doot that find it he will
Then a' that's left is to pay the bill.
Toshie's working on his Allan
Wunnerin' foo lang it wid rin on a gallon.
Say's he, 'It's nae gyan worth a damn.
I think I'll awa and hae a wee dram.
And if the morn it still winna gie a host,
I'll get the blowlamp and gie it a roast.'

Noo if yer diesel is gie'n ye trouble
See Ally Forteath, he'll come at the double.
And with all his expertise
Pumps and injectors he'll fix with ease.
He's just picked up a Fairbanks Morse
But what a red up, it couldn't be worse.
There's lots o' bits broken
And the big end is knockin'.
But efter a' this tale o' woe
He says he'll hae it at the show.
Noo doon near the end o' Cadgers Road
Lives a man in a fancy abode.
Doug Morrison is that gadgie's name,
For collecting cast iron seats he has great fame.
He's raket here and raket there
But damn, he canna fin' ony mair.
So a' you fermers better watch oot,
Or yer seats will a' end up in Doug's car boot.

Jock Baillie

Doon at the Cadger

Doon at the Cadger
Roostie workin' awa' like a badger.
He's in his shed, sittin' on the floor
On every side Rustons galore.
There's some without mags,
Ithers packed inta bags.
A fair puckle nae even painted,
And some's got him near demented.
But haud on tae yer hat,
He's jest got ane tae start.

Jock Baillie

This next poem is dedicated to the late David Murdoch, a true friend.

Davie Murdoch's Party

All dressed up like a toff
For Dallas we all set off.
To attend a party up at Craigmill
And Davie Murdoch footin' the bill.

The road to Dallas wi' sna' wisna good
All thinking, weel, we'll get some food.
Aye he's bound to have on a big roast.
But alas all we got was beans on toast.

On the table bottles of whisky,
Good stuff to make you frisky.
Heaps of vodka, enough tae full twa pails,
Jist the ticket for a' the females.

Twa or three tins export,
As weel as a half dizzen bottles o' port.
The legs o' the table war near broken
Wi' a' the wecht they were takin'.

Roostie lying on his belly,
Says Janie, 'Yer feet are awfy smelly.'
So in the fire his socks he flung,
For they smelled just like pig's dung.

As Janie sat there scratchin' her pow,
The socks baith went up in a low.
Then the gramophone it wis wound,
And abody got up wi' a bound.

'A dance,' says Davie, 'so yer partners grab.'
Says Robbie, 'Man, that's jist the very dab.
We'll hae a birl o' an eightsome reel,
So yer jackets ye'd a' better peel.'

As the nicht wore on abody got dafter.
And Doug he was hingen' frae the rafter.
Alister lookin' tae see fa else tae annoy.
Davie and Roostie awa' on some ploy.

Interferin' wi' the beds up the stairs,
The twa o' them just a gey pair.
But the clock goes on, it disna stop.
Says Robbie, 'Off tae ma bed I'll pop.'

So with baith hands on his doup
Into his bed he did loup.
And wi' a yowl he says, 'Fegs,
There is something wrang wi' ma legs!'

Says Sheila, 'A gowk ye always wis,
Wi' yer legs there is nothin' amiss.
It's Davie's bed that's tae pot.
I think I'll go and hae anither port.'

While Tosh in the bedroom next door,
Stanin' naked, the blankets on the floor.
His feet wis cauld, his twa teeth chatterin',
Thinkin', 'The morn I'll gie Davie a batterin'.'

Wishin' tae hell he had never left hame,
Says he, 'For sure a'll nae dae it again.'
End of story, I'll hae tae stop,
Or the wifey says a'll get the chop.

Jock Baillie

Davie Murdoch

Alister MacIntosh (Tosh)

This is a poem someone wrote and sent to our office. We never found out who sent it. I think it must have been someone local.

12th December 1975

If you ever come to Gairmouth
Tae hiv a look aroun'
Tak a look at Baillie's Garage
It's the greatest in the toon.
It's noo great and big

Built up wi' lots o' hard work
An' mony 'oors o' dig.

It's nae langer smelly
Green's pigs noo on top.
Come and see the building
It's bigger than the Kop.

There's Jock, Gordon, Davey,
Workin' cheils a' three.
Three country gentlemen,
All busy as the bee.

There's Ann, Jock's dochter,
Courtin' strong, I see.
A braw cheery lassie,
I'm sure you'll agree.

There's young Jock and Wullie,
Both full o' beans.
I'm sure mony a bonnie lassie
Sees them in their dreams.

But dinna forget dear granny,
Kind and generous.
Handin' oot cups o' tay.
Let's nae forget friend Sampey,
He keeps the garage clean.

Aye neat and tidy,
Ony hoosewifie's dream.

There's a' the latest gadgets.
Lots o' the newest trucks.
The reason for it a' of course
There's nae lame ducks.

There's lots o' ither workers,
Workin' nicht and day.
They're a' a happy family
At Gairmouth on the Spey.

So lift up oor glesses,
Come and hae a peek.
There's nae a better toast
Than, 'Lang may yer lum reek.'

Signed 'Cheers'

This story is about my first loan from a bank. Doris and I were on a flight returning from a holiday in Tenerife. We were sitting beside two ladies and in the conversation one lady asked me where we came from. I said we came from Elgin. I never ever said Garmouth simply because not many people have heard of it. The lady said, 'I know people from Elgin.' I then said, 'I'm not actually from Elgin, I'm from a small place called Garmouth.' She said that was where the person she knew came from. I asked what was his name, she replied, 'A banker, Ron Peterkin.' I knew right away who she was talking about. I said that I had quite a sizable business which had been started in Garmouth and that was the bank which I had used until it closed. I gave her my name and address and said to be sure and give my regards to Ron. Well, not long after there was a knock at our door and there was Ron. He was visiting relations in Elgin and decided to come and see me. After the bank in Garmouth was closed he had been transferred to a bank in Cupar in Fife but was now retired. A couple of years went by after this meeting bringing us to 2008. 1958 was the year that Baillie Brothers first made an appearance so it was our fiftieth anniversary in business. There was a big write up in some of the transport journals about us. Ron Peterkin sent me the following letter on the next page.

Ballie Brothers Set the Next
Benchmark
This is a page from the magazine
Ron Peterkin saw.

CARLOWAN,
MILLGATE,
CUPAR,
FIFE,
KY15 5EB.

30th. July, 2008.

Dear Jock,

BAILLIE BROTHERS

Many congratulations on the achievement of fifty continuous years of being in business.

Yesterday, purely by chance, our older son called to see us and presented me with a copy of an article, from a transport magazine, entitled "Baillie Brothers Set The Next Benchmark." I was delighted to see it and, of course, read it avidly. Then, while I was doing so, my mind slipped back - was it really over fifty years ago ? - to the day you came in to the Bank in Garmouth and asked me for the loan of (I "think") £100 to buy a lorry. I recollect that I said something like " you'll not get much of a lorry for that to which you answered it will do fine." I then handed over the money and you were in business, without fuss or any bother. Rather a contrast to what would happen today on receipt of a similar request!! Anyway I was delighted to read about the excellent progress of your business and it just goes to show that with a bit of hard work, and consistent application from a sound start "great oaks can grow from little acorns."

I haven't been North again for some time and in fact I have been struggling a bit health ways. Back in January I suffered what was diagnosed as two mini strokes and, as a result, I had my driving licence suspended. However, I had an examination at Ninewells Hospital, Dundee, this afternoon and I was told that I was much improved and should hear shortly from my doctor that I could set in motion the process for the return of my licence. It will certainly be a great relief for me to get it back for after driving continuously for over fifty years I found that its loss was hard to bear. Maybe I'll manage another trip north again yet, before Christmas!!?

It's now Sunday, August 3rd. and if I don't stop off and get along the road to the Post Office it will be Christmas! Anyway, this short note will perhaps show you that I have long admired your hard work and success and for now and the future all good continuing luck for you, your family and your business. I am proud to think that I had some input to its start.

Hoping that I'll manage North sometime before the end of the year and give you a call then.

Yours sincerely,

In 1986 I had to go into hospital for a prostate operation. It was a bit of a disaster and I had to go back three times to Mr. Debo. It was really very painful and I dreaded going back. Eventually I had to go back for a fourth time. This time I had a new surgeon, Mr. Gunn. He used a different method which was a complete success.

Here is a poem I wrote about it.

In the middle of nineteen eighty-six
Says I to myself, 'Now I'm in a fix.
For this old pizzle of mine
Has just stopped producing urine.'
I squeezed and pushed and farted
But I'm damned if I could get it started.
So to the doctor's surgery I did go.
Says the doctor, 'I think you are in a knot,
For your pizzle it is a' to pot.
Into hospital you must go,
There you will see a mannie called Surgeon Debo.'
So the very next day to hospital I went
And up to the male ward I was sent.
And there in the corner was my bed.
Next bed to mine was a mannie called Ned.
Then nurses appeared from every direction,
Whipped off my clothes and gave me an injection.
And then on the scene came the mannie Debo
And he says to me, 'Down to my workshop you must go.'
Then they wheeled me away on a bed on wheels,
Doon to the shed where he kept his tools.
There was the pliers, hammers and even a spade.
So there I was, doon in his den.
But what did he do to me, damned if I ken.
Up in the ward two hours efter I woke up in a hell of a temper.
For instead of a pizzle I had a tube made of plastic,
An' I am sure the damn thing was held with mastic.
The nurses were good there is no doubt.
When I misbehaved they gave me a clout.
They looked after me well, fed me three times a day.
I think for sure they wanted me to stay.
But I said, 'Not on your life, no, no, no.
I want nothing to do with Surgeon Debo.'
So that is the story of my operation.
I had to have it, I had no option.

                                                              Jock Baillie

In 2000, I contracted e.coli and was taken to Dr. Gray's Hospital Elgin. I kept getting worse and could hardly move. I managed to shuffle through to the bathroom. No wonder I had a job moving about, when I looked in the mirror I was enormous. I weighed myself and found that I was over twenty stones, I was normally only thirteen stones. My body was full of fluid, the e.coli had attacked my kidneys and they had stopped working. I found it impossible to urinate. They sent me through to Aberdeen where I got a lot worse. In fact, I lost two days because I can't remember anything about them. Doris spent one of the days with me and I have no recollection of that at all. When I did come round I was so thirsty but I was not allowed anything to drink. I was desperate to urinate but couldn't. There was a toilet in the room and the nurses kept taking me over to it but nothing happened. Then, at last just before we got to the toilet, I just exploded. Well, there was urine everywhere but that was the turning point. I began to get better every day. I remember going to the basin to wash my face and found it very difficult. I was so weak I could not lift my hands up. I had to lower my face down on to the face cloth. I then thought I would comb my hair but that beat me. I just could not lift my hands above my waist. They told me my heart had stopped twice but I'm here to tell the tale, proof they must have got it going again. I never want to go through that again. I had to attend Aberdeen Hospital a month after I got home and then every two months because my kidneys had been damaged. Happily they improved steadily and our local medical centre kept a check on me. In 2010 I was told that my kidneys were back to normal again. The doctor in Aberdeen told me that I was fortunate I didn't have to go on a dialysis machine for the rest of my life. I really consider myself to be very lucky indeed. When I went into the hospital I was getting worse and did think that I would not be coming home alive, and I was so ill I didn't really care.

A few years ago I sent off to the Army Personnel Centre for a copy of my Army Records. One form, which I had filled in when called up, asked what I intended doing when I left the army. I had answered, Haulage Contractor. I can't even remember having filled in this form, I got quite a surprise.

This is a copy.

As I write this my son has informed me that he has sold the garage side of the business, Baillie Brothers Truck Services, for a substantial amount but has retained the haulage side, Baillie Brothers Ltd., with some thirty trucks. The reason for the sale is he is approaching retirement in two and a half years and no-one in the family is interested in carrying on. He got a very good offer which might not have happened in two years time. I'm quite sorry to see it go although I think it was the right decision. Whether any of the family will be interested in carrying on with the haulage when John retires remains to be seen. I have had a great time since I decided to leave my job and start on my own in 1956, although many a time I felt like bulldozing the lot into the sea. Looking back I have enjoyed every minute of it. Even though we had quite a large business, some thirty trucks and plant hire with eight earth moving machines and eighty-three of a staff, I never mixed socially with any other business people. I didn't wine and dine anyone, nor did I allow myself to be wined and dined. The nearest I came was maybe a bottle of whisky at Christmas time to some of our best customers. Our employees all got a bottle as well. I always got on very well with my staff. All my life I have been shy but although at times I might have lost out because of it, I think it has also been my biggest asset as everyone seems to take to someone with a shy personality. I never knowingly used it to gain an advantage. I was long retired before I realized it and only found out during a conversation with a friend. He said it was the reason I had done so well. At the time I didn't think a great deal about it but later on I began to realize it was true. I was stopped for speeding three times and all I ever got was a warning. The time I was stopped for being drunk while driving, again I got off. There are a lot of other instances I can think of. I'm sure a lot of folk think I am a bit eccentric and I think they are probably right.

When I left my job in 1956, never in my wildest dreams did I think I would end up the boss of a company the size Baillie Brothers became I also have a street named after me which I thought was rather nice There are twelve houses on the site of where the garage used to be

and the street was named Jockie's Loan.

Some of the things I got up to when I retired My eldest daughter, Jane was in need of a new greenhouse. We had accumulated windows from various demolition

jobs that we had done One job especially was a school with very good

windows. I set to and built a new greenhouse for her. I built it with a wooden frame, something else we had a plentiful supply of, also reclaimed from demolition jobs.

(top left) Building the greenhouse in my workshop.
(top right) Now built and set in Jane's garden. Doris and myself standing beside it.
(bottom left) The greenhouse in use with Jane standing beside it.
I also make bird tables, there's always someone looking for one. Also wooden mannies.

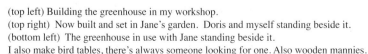

I had always fancied converting a van into a caravanette and when rust got the better of the Mercedes caravanette we'd had for twenty-seven years I bought a Mercedes minibus and set about converting it.

As well as all this I have also been restoring vintage barn engines. Also with such a large family, most of them living nearby, there is always some of them needing something to be repaired or made which I really enjoy. So you can see I have not been idle.

(top left) The minibus before conversion - One of the bigger jobs I tackled. (top right) The inside now finished.
(above left) Another view of the inside with Doris having a cup of tea.
Another project was this replica steam engine made for the grandchildren. They had great fun with it.
My grandson, Ian Birnie, driving.

I feel I should say something about my late wife who suffered a stroke and died in Doctor Gray's Hospital Elgin on the 4th of December, 2005. I and all our close family were there at the end. I was completely devastated and I do not know if I could have overcome this terrible loss without the support of my family.

Doris and I were very close, always together. Neither of us went out socially by ourselves or got involved in any of the activities in the village. She was always one hundred per cent behind me in everything I did. Without her support there would be no Baillie Brothers, that's for sure. Although I was the one that bought the bus and converted it to make it suitable to live in and then bought the prefab house from Aberdeen and rebuilt it in Garmouth and organized the building of my present house, it was Doris that made all three of them into a home. She had a hard time of it in the early years, having to carry all the water we used and having three children in nappies at the one time. I couldn't do a lot to help as I was working from twelve to eighteen hours a day.

When I started on my own Doris took over the book-keeping. She had no experience, she just learned as she went along with a bit of advice now and again from our accountant, Harry Clark, and I must say she made a first class job of it.

She also made a great job of being a mother and all my family are a real credit to her. I can take no credit for their upbringing. She was quite firm with them and if they needed a smack they got a smack, although I think it hurt their pride more than anything. When she said, 'No.' it meant, 'No.' Whereas if I said, 'No.' they usually took that to mean, 'Yes.' She didn't let me off either. I remember one Christmas, the family was all coming to us because we had a big living room, and she was getting everything ready. I was wandering about half dressed, she had told me a few times to go and get tidied up and dressed. I wasn't taking any notice so finally she said, 'For God's sake, go away where I can't see you!' Nothing ever put her up or down, she took everything in her stride. One of her pet sayings was, 'Just make the best of what you've got.' That was something we had to do quite a lot in the early years.

Eventually, in the eighties, we reaped the benefit of all out hard work and managed to go on holiday every year, sometimes for four weeks at a time and, occasionally, twice a year. Doris loved her holidays and really enjoyed herself, especially the warm countries and as long as Doris enjoyed herself, I did as well.